ABOUT THE AUTHOR

KATHLEEN PEYTON started writing at the age of nine and had her first book accepted for publication when she was fifteen. While she was at school in London, she daydreamed of owning her own pony, and so horses became the subject of many of her books.

Kathleen originally studied to become an artist, but she also continued to write and has since had more than fifty books published. She has won both the Carnegie Medal and the Guardian Children's Fiction Prize, and her best known books, the original *Flambards* trilogy, were made into a television series.

She now lives with her husband and her horses near Maldon in Essex.

To find out more about K. M. Peyton, log on to
www.kmpeyton.co.uk

NO TURNING BACK

K. M. PEYTON

USBORNE

This edition first published in the UK in 2009 by Usborne Publishing Ltd.,
Usborne House, 83-85 Saffron Hill, London EC1N 8RT, England.
www.usborne.com

First published in 2008. Copyright © K. M. Peyton, 2008

The right of K. M. Peyton to be identified as the author of this
work has been asserted by her in accordance with the
Copyright, Designs and Patents Act, 1988.

Cover photography: model supplied by Looks London Ltd./
photo by Steve Shott, background: Edward Parker/Alamy

Artwork by Ian McNee.

The name Usborne and the devices ♀ ⊕ are Trade Marks of
Usborne Publishing Ltd.

This is a work of fiction. The characters, incidents, and dialogues
are products of the author's imagination and are not to be construed
as real. Any resemblance to actual events or persons,
living or dead, is entirely coincidental.

A CIP catalogue record for this book is available from the British Library.

First published in America in 2012 AE.
PB ISBN 9780794531485 ALB ISBN 9781601302779

I

Minna walked slowly, miserably, along the beach. The autumn day was still and cool, although the sun was shining. The sea was calm, tawny-gold over the sands and mud, the horizon blending hazily into the sky, and nothing moved on the surface, not even the ship that was bringing the worst news in the world. She lay two or three miles offshore, her sails hanging, drifting on the tide.

"I hope the wind never blows. I hope they stay there forever," Minna said to herself.

But soon, she knew, they would out oars and the

slaves would start rowing and the ship would come into the fort. The commander, Theodosius Valerian Aquila, would go out on the quay to welcome it, his dark eyes glittering with joy.

Minna felt her eyes stinging with tears. "Theo, don't go! I can't live without you!" She kicked angrily at the shells that crunched beneath her bare feet. Coming the other way, collecting driftwood, was one of the village boys, Stuf. Minna scowled at him, but the amiable Stuf was not deterred.

He nodded toward the ship offshore.

"Are you invited to the party?"

"Only to work in the kitchen, what do you think? I might get to eat some leftovers if I'm lucky."

"I thought, as the commander's favorite, you might get a place at table."

He wanted her to rise to the bait. She was known in the fort as the commander's favorite because, way back, before his father had died and Theo had been forced into authority, they had been playmates together and Theo, although he was now twenty, still gave Minna access to his villa and confided in her as a friend. Quite outside Roman protocol. Not that Theo had ever been to Rome since his childhood. The cold eastern shore of Britain was the only home he really knew. Now that he was the commander of the fort, his close friendship with Minna made her mother very angry. "It's not your place to be familiar with the commander. You will get yourself a bad name. And he should know better than to encourage you."

"He doesn't encourage me!"

"He gives you access. That is enough. No one else speaks to him as you do."

But he made no move to flirt with her. He never touched her, nor made her hopeful that he might regard her as more than just a friend. He had given her a beautiful ruby ring from a hoard he had captured from pirates, which Minna had tried to think was more than just a token from a childhood playmate. But now she knew better. He had never referred to it again. Her mother, sadly, had no reason to be uneasy.

Minna loved Theo with a fierce, unrequited passion. But Theo's boss Tiberius, the tribune from Camulodunum, was sailing in now to arrange Theo's posting. Theo wanted desperately to be ordered north to where the fighting was, where the wild men from Caledonia were forever charging the great wall that the emperor Hadrian had built to keep them out.

They were enemies worth his salt. Everyone supposed Tiberius would agree to let him go. Theo was on tenterhooks to have the posting signed and sealed, which would happen over the banquet when the tribune's ship arrived on the high tide.

"Poor Minna!" Stuf said kindly, taking in her misery. "When he goes, you will forget him. Then you can marry me."

This made Minna laugh. "You! And sleep on the beach and live on stewed goose! My mother thinks I aim too high, but I don't think she would consider you, dear Stuf."

He laughed. Stuf was a beachcomber and lived off his wits. Minna liked him for his independence and good humor. He had no family but was never short of friends, being so amiable and willing to give a hand where needed. Most of the local boys were glad to join the Roman army when they were old enough, but not Stuf. "I want my own life," he said, even when the gorgeous smell of roasting boar for the soldiers' meal floated over the fort from the cookhouse door.

"You might not be the only one to regret the commander's going. He's too good a soldier to be stuck in a backwater like this. Who knows who will replace him? Some old Roman pensioner from Camulodunum, I bet, who will make us dance to his tune."

Minna groaned. "He won't like it here, not after Camulodunum."

Their fort, Othona, was miles from anywhere, even from a decent road. There was no town, only the fort stuck like a sore thumb on the flat sea marsh, home to eight hundred cavalry and a host of the usual hangers-on – local people who had gathered in the huts around the walls to trade and work for the army. Inside the fort, inside its two-meter-thick walls, were barracks, stables, granaries, mess rooms, kitchens, workshops and homes. The commander had his own villa in the center and his own servants and slaves. It was a small town in its way. But its streets were narrow, its buildings tight-packed, open space non-existent. Quarrels and gossip festered in the confinement. Minna had been to Camulodunum and knew now how other people lived, had seen for herself the great buildings: the forum and the temple of Claudius, the wide streets, the wonderful shops, the amphitheater and all the fine villas set in beautiful gardens…anyone used to all that would lose their mind in Othona.

"Perhaps he will like the seaside, the fishing...what else can I think of?"

"Nothing. Absolutely nothing."

It had been fun as children – the freedom, the creeks in the mud to dam to make mock harbors and fill with little ships made of driftwood and seaweed, to make them race on the current. Then when that palled, to turn to covering each other with mud, and then swimming it off. Always swimming; they were like fish in the sea. Theo too had been a part of it when he could get away from his lessons and then he was the leader in their adventures, getting them all into trouble. Himself especially. He was regularly beaten, mainly for skipping lessons to play. But now he could converse in several languages and do the accounts for the granaries in his head and draw maps of all the known world, read Ovid and Plato and write his own poetry. None of his playmates could write and scarcely could they read. Their native tongue came easily enough and their Latin too, because it was the language of the fort, but they couldn't understand the tongues used by many of the soldiers. They came from everywhere and many were dark-skinned from Africa. Theo's own family language was incomprehensible.

Sometimes he would laugh and speak to Minna in his native tongue, to tease, and she would pretend he was saying he loved her.

"Well, our Theodosius will be well pleased to get away from here, I'm sure," Stuf said. "The idiot is dying to go off and get killed fighting – there's no accounting for taste. Praise be to Jupiter I had more sense than to join the army like Cerdic."

Cerdic, Minna's brother, had joined up as soon as he was old enough and left his cozy home behind the blacksmith's shop for the barracks up the street. He had had a rough time, Minna knew, and was now fairly disenchanted with his choice. He was out there now mixing mortar for the wall repairs. How he felt about leaving for the North to fight the men from Caledonia Minna had no idea. He had always been a quite peaceful, if discontented, boy. As she, Minna, was discontented. If she could join the army and stay beside Theo wherever he went, even to the dangerous North, she would be happy enough.

"Cheer up, Minna!"

Stuf laughed. But kindly. He could see Minna had tears in her eyes. She was such a crazy girl! Any man who ever tamed her wild spirit would be a lucky man indeed, Stuf thought. But anyone with any sense could see that the commander was bound to look higher than Minna for a partner, although Stuf guessed that he would be hard put to find a closer soulmate. As children there had been a bond between them which had not broken. Stuf, who was so sensitive to living things, having eschewed the clangorous life of the fort, knew why Theo gave Minna a special respect. In his own way he was bound to her, although he could not admit it. It was love of a kind. Of course, Minna wanted more; she found it hard to appreciate what she already had. Stuf was deeply sympathetic.

"See if you can smuggle me out something from the banquet, Minna, if you're serving at table. I'm tired of fish. A few honey cakes and figs in wine – it's hard to pick up such goodies out here."

"I'll do my best."

She smiled. They walked along the beach together toward where Stuf had his small boat pulled up. He laid fish traps and sold his catch to housewives. He smelled of fish and salt and sweat, and wore nothing but a tattered hessian tunic with braided reeds for a belt.

"I'll see if I can find you a better tunic too. The ones the soldiers throw out are better than yours. Winter is coming, after all."

"Good girl."

Out at sea the tribune's ship was starting to move again, the sails now lowered and the oars being put to work. The tide was covering the marsh and starting to lap at the quayside on the seaward side of the fort. Minna made her way back, as she was soon to be on duty at the banquet and had to change into a decent stola. But she knew Theo would be going out on the quay to meet the ship, and if she contrived to walk home via the quay and Theo's villa she stood a good chance of meeting him. So she made her way back to the seaward side of the fort and went in at the gate that gave on to the quay. Already the guard was mustering and the ship, under its bank of sweeping oars, was making rapid progress in from the sea. She knew the slaves were chained to their oars and would not be released from their places until the ship sailed again the next day – not even then if the sea was still calm – so what had she to be miserable about? At least she had been born into a free family and even if they weren't Roman citizens they were free to do what they pleased. Cerdic would be rewarded with Roman citizenship when he left the army in twenty-five years' time, but Minna didn't think he would last that long. He was always moaning. But it had been his choice to join the army. No one was pressed. Stuf had his rights and had chosen to be what most people considered a derelict. But Minna thought he was rich in ways no one could count.

The street was crowded with soldiers making to their posts and workmen out to get a glimpse of the important visitors – anything, Minna thought, to relieve the tedium! But her pulse was quickening too, for as she came down the central street she saw that her timing was perfect, for Theo and his entourage were just coming down the steps of his villa to go out to the quay. His own bodyguard, the finest swordsmen in the army, were lined up in their best uniforms, leather and metal shining over uncommonly clean tunics, helmets gleaming, preceding the commander himself in his rarely worn white toga, symbol of authority. The snow-white drapery flattered his golden-dark skin, black hair and even blacker, alert eyes. How splendid he looked! All this to impress the tribune, to get the tribune to give in to his request to go north to where the fighting was...what an idiot he was! Minna thought. A lump came into her throat. If he smiled at her now she would burst into tears.

But he went past without seeing her in the throng, and the trumpets rang out from the ramparts as the slaves shipped their oars and the vessel glided expertly alongside the quay on the other side of the wall. Minna ran for home and was scolded by her mother for leaving it so late.

"We should be in the kitchen by now! Where have you been? Hurry now, get dressed!"

Minna scurried to make herself respectable. Theo would notice her. She brushed out the cloud of her thick hay-blonde hair that she normally confined in braids and quickly rubbed chalk into her too-bright cheeks. Not enough for her mother to notice. Then, with her mother grasping her hand, she was hurried back to the commander's villa to start work.

II

Although she tried to overhear the conversation around the banquet tables, Minna found it impossible. She was forever on the move, taking away dishes and hurrying back to the kitchen to get more. For the isolated fort of Othona, stranded on the lonely Dengie promontory on the seashore of Essex, the visit of such a large retinue was a rare occasion. Othona had been built to repel raiders from the North Sea, not to entertain visitors. It had had visits from Tiberius before, but usually in passing, from the sea, for business. He had never called, as now, with a dozen or so of his own councilors, his wife and his daughter Julia, and their servants. It was causing pandemonium in the kitchen and panic among the overworked slaves, but all were striving not to let Theo down. He was popular with everyone, not just Minna.

The atrium was ablaze with lamps and the tables sumptuously laid, the surrounding couches resplendent with gorgeous draperies. Minna knew that the finery came from the chests left behind by Theo's parents, who had returned to Rome a few years ago. Theo had never opened them since, not a man to be bothered with splendor. He only thought of his soldiers, and fighting. The beautiful Syrian glassware, the exquisite silverware and pottery sparkled in the lamplight as if rejoicing at being released for use again. Theo and Tiberius lounged on the best couch, scooping up oysters and swigging wine – although Minna noticed that Theo's wine was well diluted with water. He needed to keep his wits about him. There being no women in Theo's company to entertain them, Tiberius's wife and daughter sat together listening to the music played by two of Theo's slaves, elderly men who had elected to stay when their former employers returned to Rome. They were somewhat rusty these days, Theo having little time for music. But Minna could see they were doing their best for the two bored ladies. Feasts such as this went on for hours but it was good manners to stay awake and interested.

Minna was acutely aware of Julia, whom she had heard suggested as a possible wife for Theo. Well, thank goodness, Julia was unlikely to want to marry a man who was off to fight on the great wall against the barbarians. Minna had met Julia when she had gone on a mission to Camulodunum to summon help for the besieged Othona, and had found her a warm-hearted and friendly girl. She was eighteen, very beautiful, with a mass of reddish hair which was tonight tightly coiffed up high and stuck full of jewels. She was thin, almost angular, and active and – Minna thought – bored, like me. The last time they had met, Julia had warmly befriended her, but this time it was a little embarrassing for Minna to be in the servant's role, and Julia did not acknowledge her – which was to be expected – save once by a slight sideways smile. At least she wasn't sitting next to Theo, enchanting him with her flashing blue eyes. She scarcely glanced at him but gazed glumly into space. Her father was talking very earnestly to Theo, and as the night wore on Minna noticed that Theo's good spirits seemed to be evaporating. A scowl appeared on his face as he listened, and he made a few sharp comments, only to be steamrollered by the garrulous Tiberius. Minna was fascinated. Was Tiberius forbidding Theo to march north to fight? If only…! Whatever the tribune's instructions, it was obvious they were not to Theo's liking. But whatever they were, Theo would have to obey.

Minna was devoured by curiosity. After she had cleared away the bones of the picked venison haunches and ribs of wild boar and brought on the sweetmeats and fruits, she did her best to hover behind Theo to eavesdrop, but Benoc, Theo's personal slave, blocked her way and kicked her spitefully on the ankle. But soon he had to come into the kitchen to refill the finger bowls and find clean linen and Minna asked him: "What is that conversation all about? Theo looks angry."

"He doesn't like what's in store for him. I do though. It's great." And certainly Benoc looked happier than Minna had seen him in a long time.

"What's in store for him?"

"You'll have to ask him yourself. I'm not telling."

How mean he was!

Minna tossed her head angrily. "He will tell me. You needn't bother yourself!"

But when? she wondered. She would find it hard to contain herself until she knew.

Whatever it was, Theo's temper did not improve. He had made an effort to show good manners to his superior but it was obvious he was upset. When eventually Tiberius was ready to retire to bed and they rose from the table, the tribune threw a fatherly arm around Theo's shoulders and said, "You will thank me for this one day, my boy, never fear. It's for your own good."

"One day, but not now, sir, I'm sorry." This was a very bold remark to a superior, Minna knew, and she held her breath until she saw that Tiberius thought it amusing rather than insolent. He clapped Theo on the shoulder and said, "Show me my bed, before I drop."

Theo shouted to Benoc and the other slaves, and the whole retinue from Camulodunum was shepherded politely out to the various guest rooms and appropriated barracks. Theo stayed at the table, refilling his glass with wine, unadulterated now. Aware of his bitter mood Minna and the kitchen slaves nervously cleared the banquet tables. When they were bare they all tiptoed away except Minna. Benoc was still away seeing to Tiberius's comforts and Minna was prepared to take her chance. Theo would most likely snap her head off, but it was worth a try. She moved silently to Theo's side and stood without speaking. Her gaze was drawn helplessly to the proud profile he presented: the high brow topped with tightly curling black hair, the straight, hawkish nose, the sweet curving lips and the skin so golden-dark and clear save for the evening shadow of his beard. The black-brown eyes, veiled by long black lashes, focused – angrily – on the empty wine glass.

"Bring me more wine," he said roughly.

Minna scuttled back to the kitchen and got an amphora from the store. She brought it to the table and poured it expertly. And stayed at his side. Theo drank deeply.

"You can join me, if you like."

"I can't drink wine with you, sir."

"I'm ordering you. Take a glass." He pushed one toward her. "Sit down and hear my fate, pretty Minna. I am leaving Othona, but not with my command to fight in the North. I'm to be a pen-pusher, a bookman, an accountant. Office-bound. Rome-bidden. To run the citadel of Camulodunum."

"But you're a soldier!"

"I told him that. He laughed. He said all the great senators were in the army before they graduated to government. He said I am too clever to be a soldier. I can read and write and speak five languages. Why should I lay myself open to having my brains stoved in by a club-wielding barbarian? I am too valuable, he said. It's a promotion. I should be grateful."

Minna felt her head whirling. It was the last thing she had expected: her shock was as great as Theo's. But the shock was not accompanied by despair, but by a desperate relief that he was not going into danger and he wouldn't be far away! Camulodunum was only a few miles across the water. He wanted sympathy but it was not in her heart to give it.

"Here, sit down," he said. "Until Benoc comes back. That's one person who will be happy with the news, at least."

"And I too, that you are not going into danger."

"Oh come, Minna, you have never been afraid of danger! Sometimes I dreamed that when we went up north you could have come too and been my slave instead of Benoc. In my dream you rode Silva at my side, even into battle."

Oh, how the wine was talking! Minna felt her head spinning. Her own dream too, to have escaped the fort when Theo left and followed the baggage train...but never in her dream had she seen herself at his side, on her beloved pony Silva! Even dreams did not stretch so far. She wondered if she had heard correctly. She was not used to undiluted wine.

"I am talking out of place," Theo said, smiling suddenly. "Poor Minna! What can we do except obey orders? We have no choice. I shall serve out my apprenticeship as office boy, learn how to command scribes and money counters, pay bills, listen to peasants' complaints, put up my sword..."

His smile died. Minna knew he was a superb swordsman. She could not picture him as a governor of civil servants instead of soldiers.

"What happens to your command here? Does the cohort go with you?"

"Octavius takes my place. I go alone."

So dour old Octavius would replace Theo's popular rule. A much older man, Octavius had been soured by young Theo's being made commander above himself and was very unpopular. Minna's brother Cerdic would stay, along with his horse Silva, who Minna always thought of as her own, for all he lived in the army barracks. She had rescued him as a foal when he had been dumped out on the marsh as too weak to be bothering with. Cerdic had helped her, against his will, and she had rashly promised he could keep the animal if it lived. It had grown into the best horse in the whole cavalry and Cerdic now rode him as his army mount. But there was a bond between Silva and Minna, who had raised him by hand, and Minna knew she had Silva's devotion. It grieved her bitterly that he now belonged to the Roman army and, worse, was ridden by ham-fisted Cerdic, who had no feeling for horses. If he had been ridden by Theo she would have been happy, but Theo, even with his authority, was too decent to order the horse from Cerdic, breaking a promise. So, at least, Silva would stay. Minna often rode him out when he was not wanted on army exercises. But it was quite likely that Octavius would forbid this favor. Theo's rule was unorthodox, not at all to the letter of the Roman law. The men loved him for it and were unlikely to prefer Octavius's strictness.

Benoc came back and scowled at Minna. Theo started to drink himself into oblivion and Minna knew she must leave him to Benoc. She backed away and went out of the villa into the cold night to make for home, the cramped quarters behind her father's blacksmith shop by the west gate. Her mother would be back already, waiting to scold her. Minna thought the cold night air would clear her foggy brain. She would realize that Theo's words, about her riding by his side into battle, were just the waffle of inebriation.

But they sang in her head, over and over. She could not get the words out of her mind.

III

When Minna's mother heard the news of Theo's future she was pleased.

"At least the poor boy will not be going into danger, nor taking Cerdic with him either! That's wonderful news. Thank the gods for that!"

Although Theo was the commander of the fort, Minna's mother still remembered him as a boy playing on the marshes with her own two children and tended to speak of him as "that poor boy." In her maternal way, she had always thought his upbringing very hard. But in his presence she – unlike Minna – was the perfect servant. She was forever scolding Minna for her familiarity with him. But now she saw salvation: with his departure Minna would stop hankering after her hero and come down to earth.

"Your father has spoken to Esca's parents. They are happy about a betrothal, fortunately. We thought they might consider you too wild to make a good wife, but we have convinced them you are growing out of your childish ways. We can have the wedding quite soon now nothing stands in the way."

"I don't want to marry Esca!"

"That really doesn't come into it, Minna, as well you know. Esca is a perfectly decent young man with good prospects. What more do you want? He's not cross-eyed or bow-legged, not even pimply, and his parents are a respectable couple. We were prepared for them to turn you down as not good enough."

"A pity they didn't!"

"If you don't behave well toward him your father will give you a good beating, you know that. So grow up and be sensible."

Minna knew she had no ground to stand on in this argument. She was lucky not to have been married off a year or two earlier. She was quite old now, at fourteen. Her parents had been lenient with her. She could see that they were happy that the army was staying put so Cerdic would still be around, and her mother was clever enough to point out that this would mean that Minna's dear pony Silva would not be leaving the fort.

But the thought of Theo leaving was so overwhelming that she thought it hardly mattered now who she married. If it wasn't Theo – and she had always known that was impossible – any stupid boy would do.

This did not stop her from saying hopefully, "I wouldn't mind marrying Stuf."

Her mother broke into a gale of laughter. "And live in a hut on the beach and eat fish all your life? Oh come, Minna, you're surely not that stupid?"

And she put her arm around Minna and gave her a quick hug.

"Be a good girl and don't make a fuss. It happens to us all. Even your beloved Theo will have to marry whoever those above him decree. It's the way of the world."

Minna could not even begin to think of Theo marrying. It was far too painful. Nor could she bring herself to pass the time of day with Esca. He worked outside the fort in his father's butcher's shop, a lanky boy of eighteen with a flat Germanic face and pale blue eyes. He had never wanted to join the army and had little ambition that Minna could see. He spent his spare time larking and drinking with his mates, not hunting boar or usefully fishing or doing anything brave and manly. Minna did not see how she could possibly respect him.

The whole community was in a great ferment with the news of Theo's departure. Both the army and the civilians were distressed at losing him. They had been prepared for him to go, leading his army to do battle, but to go alone to Camulodunum to be more civil servant than soldier was a great disappointment. What a waste! was the general opinion. The governing bodies in big towns were loathed by the ordinary working man because they levied such vast taxes. The one good thing about living in back-of-beyond Othona was that government officials largely left them alone. Now Theo was going to be one of "them." He deserved better! But they understood he had no choice. And matters were not helped by the thought of bad-tempered old Octavius taking his place. The young soldiers hated him.

When Minna next met her brother Cerdic they unloaded their sorrows on each other, for once in accord. Cerdic, off duty, had slipped into his old home and found Minna at work sewing army tunics. This was her mother's job and Minna worked with her (not by choice, needless to say). After he had helped himself to a honey cake and a handful of dates out of the kitchen, Cerdic came and sat by Minna.

"A bad business, eh? We were all looking forward to marching north and getting into a few skirmishes. And now what? Deadly Octavius – guard duty and drill, and more drill, and more guard duty, no larks unless you want a flogging. Everyone knows he's just holding on until his pension's due. I've a good mind to desert."

"Don't be so stupid. Where would you desert to?"

"There are old tribes up the coast who like fighting. They'll take anyone, no questions asked. Some of the boys are thinking about it, when Theo goes."

"You'll end up as a slave if you're caught! It's much too dangerous, you idiot."

Spoiled by his mother, a favorite of Theo's in his boyhood, always longing to join the army, Cerdic forever wanted the next thing. Being in the army had been a bitter disappointment to him. The grim reality of training and hard work had not been at all to his liking, and – as a spoiled youth, a stripling Briton – he had been given a rough time by the professional stalwarts from all the far-flung corners of the Roman world that made up Theo's command.

Seeing him lounging there, a slender, handsome young man in his fine uniform, Minna wished she could marry a soldier instead of the ham-faced Esca. Disaffected he might be, but Cerdic cut an impressive figure with the sword on his hip, which she knew perfectly well he had been taught to use to good effect. He had always liked hunting in the forest, chasing deer and wild boar, and breeding hunting hounds from his dog Mel, which he sold for good sums. His own favorite hound, Fortis, lived in the barracks with him and was always at his heels when he was off duty. He loved Fortis as Minna loved Silva.

"I'll come back with you to see Silva," Minna said, putting down her work. "What shall we do, Cerdic, with Theo going? I shall die!"

"Yeah, the whole army is pretty sick about it, not just you."

"And I'm to marry Esca, did you know?"

"By Jupiter, poor Esca! No, I didn't know. I assumed you would go chasing off to Camulodunum after Theo like the foolish girl you are."

"That's the same as you saying you're going to desert. What we would *like* to do…that doesn't come into it. It's only what we've *got* to do."

The disgruntled siblings walked back to the barracks together. Minna only went in the barracks when all the soldiers were out and, now, apart from a couple of guards coming in off duty, the place was empty. All the horses were in and the warm smell of dungy bedding and fresh hay soothed Minna's discontent. At least she would still be close to Silva, her only solace.

Silva whinnied softly as Minna appeared, recognizing her step before she came into sight. Minna went into his stall and laid her cheek thankfully against the hard, sleek neck.

"Oh, Silva, what am I going to do?" And at the awful thought of marrying Esca she started to cry, pressing her face into Silva's dark mane. Even Silva, she knew, could be taken away if she was unlucky. A mere chattel of the Roman army, he could easily be promoted to a rider more senior than Cerdic or, if a local dignitary demanded him, Octavius, unlike Theo, would not hesitate to do a deal. Silva was by far the best horse in the cohort, a well-grown dark gray stallion of some fourteen hands – tall by army standards. Most of their horses were native-born and their riders' feet swung only just clear of the ground. But Silva had been sired by an imported Barbary horse, which had stamped itself in his elegant head with its fine muzzle and large, intelligent eyes, the high tail carriage and the good hard legs. The army found it difficult to breed larger horses, having to import stallions from Gaul, which, besides being very expensive, often did not result in very good crosses. Few of the fine Barbary stallions from North Africa made it as far as England, being appropriated along the way by greedy horsemasters, so Silva was something of a rarity. Minna had raised him herself and kept him in her care until he was old enough to be ridden, and he answered to her as he answered to no one else. Even the old hard-bitten Roman horsemaster acknowledged that Minna had a magic way with horses.

It was a relief to let the tears flow, her arms around Silva's neck, her face buried in his mane. His stall was her dearest refuge, away from her parents' nagging, secure in the horse's loyalty. Her future was grim, and she couldn't see any way out of it. But the worst, with Theo going, was the risk to Silva now Octavius was in charge. Octavius could well decide to take him as his own mount, and that would be a disaster, as he was a terrible ham-fisted rider, far worse than Cerdic.

Even if it would mean the horse leaving Othona, it might be better, Minna decided, if Theo took him as his own mount to Camulodunum. She would ask Theo! But the pain of losing Silva would be crucifying. She sobbed bitterly, alone in the stable, and Silva turned his head and pushed his muzzle at her as if he understood her grief. Minna could not make up her mind what to do. The despair washed over her. It probably wasn't in her power to change anything, she knew, for getting an audience with Theo was difficult. Maybe she could catch Benoc to pass a message. But did she want Silva to go?

"Oh, Silva, what shall I do? When Theo goes – and you – I might as well be dead!"

She told herself that if things had gone right and

Theo had been sent north with his army Silva would have departed anyway, but somehow that now seemed a fate she could have lived with. It was what she had been expecting and had almost prepared herself for. Bad enough, but not as bad as the way things had turned out. Deep down she knew that the prospect of marrying Esca was worse than even those dreadful things and that was why the tears would not stop. To be a wife to that oaf, to work in the butcher's, to bear stupid babies – even die in the act, it was common enough – never be free again to gallop along the shore with the rain on her face and the wind in her hair... Minna wailed, oblivious to who might hear her.

Nobody did. Only the horses in their stalls shifted wearily and jackdaws cackled in the roof. Winter was setting in and the wind was blowing hard from the east, black clouds pouncing across the hard, bright stars. The lookouts up on the ramparts were no doubt crouched under the wall, wondering why they bothered. What could be seen on a night as dark as this? The force of the sea was spent silently on the great tracts of marsh and mud that stretched far offshore, and only the smell of it told it was there, the tide low, the moon a hidden, thin crescent. The soldiers would be back from the drinking dens shortly. Minna gave Silva a last, hiccuping kiss and slipped out, holding her cloak tightly around her. The wind whistled down the narrow road between the buildings. She had to pass the commander's fine villa on the way home. Lights shone inside but his guard was on the portico and Minna knew it was impossible to gain entry. What did Theo care for her anyway? The lovely Julia would be awaiting him in Camulodunum. Still choked with tears, Minna hurried home.

IV

Theo departed three days later. Minna never got a chance to speak to him, not daring to broach his guards, and could only watch helplessly with the rest of the crowd as he came out of his villa to board the fort ship the *Othona* to leave for Camulodunum. The whole army was lined up on the parade ground and Theo walked slowly through the ranks with Octavius, stopping many times for a private word of farewell, mainly to the older soldiers who had served under his father. Some of these soldiers could remember him being born. Minna knew that most of them had been eagerly looking forward to going off under his command to fight and they were as bitterly disappointed as she was to lose him. She wasn't surprised at Cerdic's saying that some of the younger ones were talking of deserting.

She pressed forward in the crowd to see the affecting military farewell. It was a bright, cold day and Theo's cuirass and helmet glittered in the sunlight with Benoc's polishing; the lovely jeweled sword that he could use to such good account swung on his hip. He cut a splendid figure. "What a waste," everyone was saying, not just Minna. The only person to be pleased was Benoc, the devoted slave. The civilian milieu was to his taste. Minna wondered then if he would have followed Theo to fight. He might have absconded, even at the risk of being put to death if he had been caught. Or perhaps his love for Theo would have kept him loyal; Minna had no way of knowing. As always, she was jealous of Benoc for his closeness to Theo. (Of a slave, for the gods' sake – was she insane? Sometimes she thought she was.)

So Theo went aboard the ship and the trumpets rang out on the ramparts as the sail was hoisted to the fair southwesterly breeze. He took his slaves and servants and his personal bodyguard. The ship slipped eagerly into the North Sea and headed across the wide Blackwater estuary toward the mouth of the river that led inland to Camulodunum. Minna walked alone out of the fort to the farthest point of the Dengie and stood watching until the ship was out of sight. He had not said goodbye to her, not even searched for her in the crowd to give a last smile. She had his ring to remember him by, but she thought he would forget her now. The lovely – and eligible – Julia was waiting for him in Camulodunum and was probably being prepared by her parents to accept him in marriage, just as Minna was being ordered to marry Esca. None of them in this Roman-riven life could do as they pleased!

After Theo's departure the bright weather gave way to a cold rain that blew in from the North Sea. It was tears for Theo's departure, Minna thought, to match her own. She had known she was going to miss him, but she didn't realize how dreary the days would become without having him just to look at as he went about his command, without the delicious prospect of him stopping to smile at her, or speak. And with Octavius on the rampage, giving rein to his new authority, there was no chance of riding Silva, even when the troops were out and the horses left in the stable. If he found out, she knew there would be a severe punishment. This would redound on her parents and they might lose their living. She couldn't risk that.

They were going ahead with preparations for her marriage, and that seemed to occupy her mother to the exclusion of everything else. The talk was all of where the ceremony would take place, what they would wear, what they would eat, what musicians could be hired. Women neighbors were in the house gossiping all day. Minna was measured for her wedding tunic and when her mother had sewn it Minna had the task of embroidering it. Every stitch was stabbed with hate and despair. When Esca came near her, grinning, Minna wanted to scream.

"I can't!" she sobbed to her mother. "I can't!"

"You can and you will," her mother said grimly. "Do you think you're the first girl to think like this? Or boy, too, for that matter? It is something that has to be faced in this life. Esca's family is prosperous and well-respected and where else will you find a boy as suitable? You'll scarcely be leaving home, only moving a few doors down the street. I will be at hand to help you with your children – you should consider yourself lucky it is all so painless for you! You're lucky you haven't been chosen by some old man whose wishes we would be bound to respect – think of that and be grateful."

Minna knew only too well that this was a common enough fate, especially among the ruling classes who used marriage between families to cement business deals and land ownership. She stopped sobbing but, later, when her parents hosted a supper with Esca and his parents, to discuss wedding details, she felt such despair that she vowed there and then that the wedding would not take place. How she would manage to avoid it she had no idea, but avoid it she would, even if it meant running away and hiding in the forest and living off mushrooms, or hiding on a ship and getting taken far away to another country.

Perhaps, if she had never met Theo, she could have stomached Esca's flat cheerful face. But he was boring, brainless, in Minna's opinion. Whatever would they talk about together? She could talk with Stuf, with

Cerdic, even Benoc! And with Theo, forever. But across the table when they hosted Esca's family, she found they had no words in common. He only knew about butchering and drinking. He was so brainless he could hardly speak Latin in spite of it being in his ears all day long. His father was astute and a good friend of her own father's, but Esca took after his dreary Gallic mother, whom even Minna's mother found hard going. The two of them, mother and son, were peasants. Her children would be flat-faced and brainless. She couldn't!

Thank the gods there was a slight hold-up in the plans owing to the ill-health of the old grandmother, who was near death. Esca's family wanted to see her off first, in case she chose to die just when the wedding was about to swing into action. There were also the stars to consult, according to Esca's mother, and the blessings of various gods and goddesses to plead for. Fortunately all this meant procrastination. At the rate it promised to go on, Minna thought, with luck it would be next spring before her fate descended. She thought long and hard about how to avoid it, but knew it was impossible unless she ran away. That idea was like a blank, brick wall.

One day she asked Stuf about rowing her across the river. There were plenty of settlements over there: she had seen them. The area was farmed and much more homely than the dreary marshland of the Dengie that she called home. Surely someone would employ a skilled seamstress? She knew she was good. Her mother had seen to that.

But Stuf, down-to-earth and honest, said, "Much as I would like to help you, it is bound to be discovered that I rowed you, and where would that leave me? Pitched out into exile, for sure. I don't want that."

Minna sighed. "No, I suppose so."

And besides, such an escape would mean leaving Silva behind. Forever. And Silva was the only real friend she had now. When Octavius was safely in his villa at night and the soldiers out drinking, she would creep into the stables and talk to Silva. Quite often she sobbed into his soft mane and if he was lying down she lay down beside him and told him all her troubles. She knew that he trusted her completely. It made the thought of leaving him all the harder to bear.

"I can't go without you!"

*   *   *

One evening Cerdic told her that they were doing pack drill the day after: thirty miles with full kit at fast marching pace. Octavius had told them they were getting flabby. The horses were to be left behind, save for that of Octavius. He would ride. This exercise was common enough, but when Theo had ordered it he had walked too, and carried kit, the same as his men. Minna decided it would be a good opportunity to take Silva out. Wait until the cohort was well clear, and then she would find Silva and take him out along the beaches, just like old times. She would make some excuse to her mother to leave the house, or with luck her mother would send her on an errand. She went to bed happily for once. She so rarely got the chance to do this, these days! Riding Silva was her only release now, in her boring life. She felt very sorry for herself.

The next day the cohort marched out, sour-faced, into a grim winter's day. Cerdic, on his way out to the parade ground, caught Minna's arm and said, "Octavius was going to take Silva! I told him Silva was tender in front – I said he had a bruised foot. It was the first thing that came into my head. So the old man shrugged and said, 'Next time then. He's too good for you.'"

Cerdic's eyes were wide with indignation. But to Minna his words struck a chill! Silva was *hers*! Technically he belonged to the Roman army – Theo had said so, in spite of the fact that the Roman army had thrown him out as a foal. But Theo, having said that, had allocated the horse to Cerdic and had turned a blind eye to Minna "borrowing" him. It was now obvious that those days were over. Minna felt that her miseries about the impending marriage were as nothing compared to the thought of Octavius taking Silva for his own. Shaking with fury, she ran down the street to the stables. The barracks were deserted. The only soldiers left behind were the guard and the lookouts and they merely nodded to her, used to her riding out on Silva.

Silva was eating his morning hay and turned his head eagerly to greet her, his nostrils quivering with pleasure. He was so beautiful, his winter coat coming through dark as pewter, shining with good health…

"I shall never let Octavius take you, never!" She would have let Theo take him, that was different, but he had never asked. How she was going to stop Octavius she had no idea. "He is a pig, Silva. He rides like a peasant. We must think of something."

All she could think of was to lame Silva on purpose, but that was so cruel she put it out of her mind. She found his bridle and was soon leading him out into the barrack yard. She would take him out along the beach and something would come into her head – there must be an answer. There was an answer to everything if one thought long and hard enough, she decided – even if she hadn't yet come up with how to avoid marrying Esca.

She stopped at her house to collect her heavy cloak – her mother was out, luckily, else she would have had to have ridden on. Her mother didn't approve of her taking Silva, but hadn't actually forbidden it, remembering only too well the devotion with which Minna had nursed the pony as a foal. Hugging the cloak around her she trotted fast out of the west gate before the inattentive guard could stop her and cantered on along the road. Away in the distance she could see the tail-end of the marching cohort, so she turned away toward the sea, taking one of the firm paths over the swampy ground that she knew so well. Ahead of her stretched the wide estuary where the tide was rising, pushing its way against the strong wind which was blowing streamers of spray across the water. Minna's eyes watered in the cold, but Silva went eagerly, head up, the wind blowing his mane out like a banner. His long ears were pricked, his bearing proud and elegant – no wonder Octavius wanted him! Octavius wasn't such a fool, after all. Minna rode the pony into the water where the beach was firm. His hooves crunched the shell bed underfoot. Only the marsh stretched ahead, sliding into the sea, and around the point the whole ocean opened out, empty of any signs of life. Very little shipping braved sailing during the winter months. The fort rested, waiting for the coming of the spring when the invaders set sail again. The dreary route marches kept the men fit and occupied. They hated them, unsurprisingly.

How few people did what they wanted to in this life, Minna was thinking – when she came across a little scoop in the shingle and, in the shelter of a stunted excuse for an oak tree, hunkered down in the scoop, she found Stuf. He had a little fire going, sheltered by a discarded broken shield, and a fish was cooking on a wooden skewer. The only person she knew who led his own life…but then, how many people wanted to live like Stuf? Yet he looked up at her with his wide, ready smile.

"Minna! Playing truant?"

"They've gone on a route march, poor things."

"Yes, I saw them. And you wonder why I don't join the army!"

Sliding off Silva and dropping down beside Stuf, Minna found that the little indentation was enough to provide shelter; the fire burned steadily. She told him about Octavius wanting Silva.

"He'll get what he wants, you know that," Stuf said grimly.

"What shall I do?" Minna's voice came out in a wail, like the gulls' voices swooping overhead. "Marrying Esca, losing Silva – I might as well die!"

"Don't be so silly." Stuf turned his fish carefully. He wore only an old tunic and a hessian cloak, a tattered sack, yet he looked as comfortable as a man sitting in a heated dining room. Tempering her voice she said more steadily, "What shall I do then? You know how to turn life to your own advantage – look at you! If I were half as clever as you, I could do what I wanted, like you. But I can't think how."

"I can," Stuf said.

"Tell me."

"You have to go away."

"Yes, I've thought that. But you wouldn't help me across the water. Where else would I go?"

"To Theo, of course, in Camulodunum. It's not far, on Silva, a day's ride."

Minna scowled. "Do you think I haven't thought of that? But how can I? He never said a word to me about my going there. If I went, it would be throwing myself at him. I would be demeaning myself."

"Not to jump in his bed, stupid. Just to ask for shelter, a menial job, a shed for Silva. Anything. Of course he would look after you, he's a friend, isn't he?"

Minna's head spun. She had already thought to go away, but to go to Theo seemed like asking too much of the gods. Yet Stuf spoke of it as just a sensible idea. It was, when one thought about it carefully. Even if Theo had already forgotten her and wouldn't be all that pleased to see her, he wouldn't turn her away, she knew that. She could even offer him Silva, then Silva would have the job he deserved. Silva was too good for her, but if he belonged to Theo he would want for nothing. His future in Octavius's insensitive hands was grim. He did not behave well for a bad rider and would be punished. These thoughts chased each other around her head. She squatted down and watched Stuf eat his fish. He didn't offer her any.

"Perhaps I could…" She faltered. "When should I go? Soon? Before a date is fixed for my wedding, perhaps."

"Now, idiot. This minute. Once Octavius takes Silva he'll put him in the villa stable and you won't get hold of him then. You've the whole day ahead of you, you've got your thick cloak with you. What more do you want? Look, you can take my knife. I can always get another. To protect yourself, if you need to. And I've got cheese and an egg. You can have them."

Minna was speechless. She felt as if Stuf had felled her with a blow on the head.

"And don't say you can't." Stuff caught the smoking fish flesh as it fell off the bone and stuffed it into his mouth. "You know your way. You've ridden it before," he mumbled through the fish. "I will tell your parents what you've done so they won't send out a search party. I won't tell them it was my idea, though. I will tell them I advised you against it. They might ask me to dinner." He laughed.

Minna sat as if frozen in the little hollow. Silva, casting around for something to eat, spat out some seaweed and tossed his head impatiently.

Stuf looked at her, amused. "You asked."

The idea somersaulted around in Minna's head. After the first shock, it seemed eminently sensible, but very hard to accept. Now! This minute! To ride away from her warm home and fierce but loving mother…

"You take your horse," Stuf said. "What more do you want?"

"Go to Theo?" she whispered.

The name was magic to her. To be by Theo, with Silva at her side – was there anything she wanted more? She couldn't think of anything.

She laughed suddenly. "You are so clever, Stuf. Like an oracle. You have all the answers. You are the cleverest person I know. Of course I will go."

Stuf groped in a sack of his meager possessions and pulled out a small but wicked army knife. It was in a sheath on a belt.

"Take this. You might need it. But be careful with it. If you fall off it might stick in you if you don't wear it right."

"I don't fall off."

"I hope you don't have to use it." He looked a little anxious now, seeing that she was jumping at his suggestion. "There are quite a few bunches of brigands up along the coast – Britons, misfits, deserters, Germans – they gang together to plunder and give the Roman administration headaches. Try not to meet any. They take rich women and hold them for ransom."

"I'm not rich and no one will pay for me."

"No, but they might like your horse."

"Come with me!"

"No. I don't look for adventure."

Minna got up and took Silva's bridle. Stuf gave her a leg-up, then rummaged in his bag again and pulled out a hard-boiled duck egg and a piece of stale cheese. Minna took them and stuffed them in the pocket of her cloak. Silva's bare back was warm and comforting to her cold legs. She looked down regretfully at Stuf as she held in the now anxiously curvetting horse.

"Goodbye, Stuf. Thank you. You are a good friend."

"Be careful. Look out for those brigands. Keep your eyes peeled."

"Yes, I will."

And she sat tight as Silva sprang around and plunged into an eager canter back along the beach. Her head was still spinning, but with joy rather than fear, aware that in that great bound she was on her way to freedom, the freedom she craved. She could not believe how quickly her world had turned upside down. But as the blood pounded in her heart she knew it was from fear rather than joy. She was throwing over her safe dull life for who knew what? But Silva was feeling his freedom too, and his hot excitement matched her own as they careered along the edge of the wild sea away from Othona.

V

After her initial wild gallop along the shore, Minna pulled Silva back to a walk, her head whirling. Whatever was she doing? She could not believe what an idea Stuf had put into her head! To leave home, her parents, her life in the fort, to seek out Theo – had she lost her mind? Or was it the only way – once the idea was in her head – to escape her marriage to Esca? She rather thought it was. She kept the enthusiastic Silva to a walk while she tried to calm her mind, blown away by Stuf. The cold wind buffeted her, making her aware of the warm den that was her home in the fort, of her mother's love, of everything she knew so well and was about to throw away for a dream. Or was it a dream? What was wrong with dreams?

As Silva pulled eagerly at the bit, Minna looked up and caught sight of the tail-end of the cohort on their route march. She was catching up to them and soon they would see her if they took a glance behind. If she was to go on, she would have to overtake them, detouring inland to go around them, a difficult way along the edge of the forest. They were following the shore, marching westward, the same way she must take to cross the river. She knew the way well enough, if she were to go on, but it would be arduous. Soldiers with sharp eyes might pick her out unless she kept within the trees. How lucky that Silva's winter coat was still dark: in the gray daylight he would be hard to pick out. And even if they did see her, what could they do?

The tempering of her speed gave her time to sort out her brain, which still whirled with coming to terms with what she was doing. She told herself she could go on, thinking about what was best to do – she could always turn back in an hour or two if her courage failed her. The way was rough and Silva had to pick his way in and out of the trees and through thick scrub, and while they gradually overtook the marching men Minna was trying desperately to justify this action. Luckily, the more she thought about it the easier it was. The threat of Octavius taking Silva was even worse than her having to marry Esca. The two things together were unsupportable. So by the time she had cleared the marching soldiers and could get back on the road again, well ahead of them, she felt her flight was well justified. Stuf was a bright boy and it was his idea, after all. Believing in what she was doing didn't make it any less terrifying, but she felt better about it after a few miles. The walls of Othona had long disappeared in the murk and now, with growing confidence in what she was doing, she knew that she wouldn't mind if she never saw them again.

Of course, she was now a thief and a girl alone in a dangerous world. Single girls without an escort did not ride the winter roads on a beautiful horse. She pulled the cloak up high over her thick blonde hair and at one point stopped to smear mud on her face. The few peasants she passed gave her no more than a curious glance. A fine, bitter sleet was driving in from the sea and nobody was in the mood to stop and ask questions. The home hearth beckoned but she steeled herself to resist the memory. Hunching herself, head down, she kept her face turned into her hood, scowling, and trotted on briskly. The road was long and there were few settlements on it. She had to follow the river some twenty miles inland to its crossing point before she could turn back and head north for Camulodunum. What was only a few miles by sea was tenfold by land, and dark would come early. She doubted whether she would find lodging for the night, considering how few and poor the occasional hovels were. Stuf, that you were with me! her heart cried out – Stuf could make himself a home anywhere. If only he had come with her! She was frightened now, and the wind and the rain buffeted her, but she could only ride on. The decision was taken – for now – she comforted herself.

Silva covered ground fast and Minna came within sight of the settlement where the river crossing was, just as the light was fading. She didn't like approaching the settlement in the dusk – much better to ride out in the morning when people would be going on their business – so she started to look for some sort of shelter to spend the night in. But the landscape was as bleak as at Othona itself, extensive marshland seamed with deep drainage ditches running into the river on her right hand and to her left just scrubby flat grazing. The settlement itself was on a hill and a few lights gleamed faintly, but she knew there was no lodging house there: it was too far from a main road. Even if there had been, she had no money, and only Roman civil servants and dignitaries used mansios in any case. It was a ditch for her, or the shelter of some scrub or trees. It was Silva she felt sorry for more than herself; he was used to a stable and straw for a bed.

She turned off the road and made for a stand of trees. They were stunted from the wind but promised a slight shelter and there was grazing of a sort, and a bit of a bank. She got under the trees and slipped off Silva's warm back.

"Poor boy! You've got to suffer along with me. Just for now."

She took the bit out of his mouth so that he could graze and fixed it so that he was tethered by the reins. It was no use giving him the option to wander far – he would just have to go hungry, like herself. Stuf's offering of cheese and the duck egg was quickly eaten, then all she had to do was wrap the wet cloak tightly around her and lie down under the bank. The ground was soft enough, thick with autumn leaves, but she was cold and frightened at what she was doing and thought only to get through the night, somehow. To sleep would be luxury. And she was very aware of Silva's misery as he stood with his tail clamped down against the drizzle, his stomach rumbling with hunger. The night was very dark, the wind bringing the strong smell of the sea and, as always, the sense of danger. No one slept safe by the shore these days, not while men from harder lands were forever coming across the sea to look for rich pickings, to make homes and wealth. It was always so, but Minna had rarely slept away from the safety of the fort. Its walls were the thickness of two men lying head to head, and within its compass the strongest wind was but a zephyr. Normally the smell of woodsmoke and roasting meat accompanied her dreams when she went to bed, warm in a snug of animal skins and wool covers in the room behind her father's forge – how she longed for the comfort now! She wept for what she was doing, and had to call up visions of Esca's crude person to shore up her confidence – to think of lying in her cozy bed with Esca! The thought was enough to make her shivers bearable, to stiffen her resolve. But the night was long and terrible and if she slept it was only to awaken with horror at the animal sounds and scuffles in the shrub, and the cackling of geese out on the marsh as if disturbed by marauders. Not a star showed, nor any sign of a moon, and dawn was late and miserable, a tattered streak of opal-gray across the river.

Minna set off again on an eager Silva – as eager as his rider to put away the miserable night. They rode into the settlement and found few people out early, only some animal drovers and reed cutters who looked up curiously but without animosity. The road here was busier, as it crossed in all directions, and after Minna had forded the river she took the road that followed it back much the same way as she had come. She knew the big road from Londinium lay to the north but she preferred to take a lesser road to the east, quieter and perhaps less dangerous.

How different it was once clear of the marshes! Although she had ridden this way before after visiting Camulodunum, she was quite unused to this pleasant undulating countryside of woodland and pasture, dotted here and there with small homesteads. There was little of the scrub she was used to, no stunted, wind-crippled dwarf trees, but great stands of oak and elm; no wild boar but contented pigs scavenging for acorns. The smell of the sea receded and although the drizzle and the wind persisted, it seemed almost friendly compared with the night before.

Minna rode on, desperately hungry, still cold, wet and weary, still deeply worried about what she was doing but more determined by the minute. The thought of seeing Theo again warmed her, even as the water-laden cloak flapped forlornly against her legs and her teeth chattered between her lips.

But it seemed that she would have to spend another night out, for the way was not clear and she got lost several times. The people she asked the way of were friendly enough, but very curious, and two of them warned her to look out for the Cunobelin scavengers.

"Cunobelin?"

She knew that was the name of a British king who ruled in the area before the Romans came, a very long time ago.

"It's a gang of madmen that roam around here. Anti everything Roman. It's an excuse to go on the rampage, just for the fun of it. They say they're descended from

Cunobelin – well, who isn't, if you go back that far? They're thieves. They won't kill you but they'll take your horse. So be careful, girl."

An old man gave her a hunk of bread along with the warning, and Minna comforted herself by thinking that Silva could outpace any stupid thief that might stand in his way. Take her horse! The idea chilled her even further and she rode on faster, hopeful of making Camulodunum before nightfall. But soon she gave up hope of reaching the town before dark and started looking around for a shelter for the night again.

Coming along a well-worn track through woodland she saw a glimmer of light through the trees to her right. There seemed to be a glade – possibly a cottage, she thought, with an outhouse if she was lucky. So far people had been friendly enough. She pulled Silva to a halt and sat listening, aware of the now not unfamiliar knot of apprehension tightening in her chest. Why was she so scared? But she knew her strength and resolve were ebbing fast, cold and hungry and exhausted as she was. She had covered most of the distance – so near to Theo's protection but – at this moment – so far!

Silva decided for her by turning off the track toward the light. His ears were pricked and suddenly he whinnied. He stopped, stamped a hoof and whinnied again. Peering into the gloom, frightened now, Minna made out a horse tethered to a tree and, beyond, a group of men sitting around a fire. A smell of cooking wafted to her nostrils. The horse whinnied back to Silva and Minna knew she was discovered. One of the men jumped to his feet.

Minna spun Silva around.

"Not so fast there!" a voice shouted.

But Minna was taking no chances. These could be the people that might take her horse! She kicked her heels into Silva's sides and drummed him urgently into a gallop. But as she did so a figure leaped from the group around the fire and ran for the tethered horse. It jerked the rope free, vaulted onto the horse's back and swung around in pursuit. This took no longer than the time it took for Silva to get into his full stride. One glance back showed Minna that she was in deep trouble, and all she had to depend on now was Silva's speed.

VI

Fast as he was, Silva was tired and hungry and on unfamiliar ground. He was attracted to the company of another horse, not used to being on his own, and his gallop was half-hearted. Minna was exhausted and hadn't the strength to convey her urgency to Silva. All she could do was drum her heels into his sides, clutch frantically at his mane as he followed the twisting path through the thick forest and duck her head as the low branches came at her. Her fear choked her. The man had only to push her off Silva's back and take his bridle, and she had no way of preventing it.

The forest was thinning and to her dismay she was quickly out onto open ground. The path was clearly trampled over a large sward of grazing and she made for another stand of woodland some quarter of a mile ahead. Perhaps if she reached that she might have a chance to hide, but the sound of her pursuer's hooves was getting nearer and nearer. A glance over her shoulder showed a dark chestnut horse, easily as tall as Silva, gaining ground fast. It was no rough pony but a horse of quality – no wonder Silva couldn't shake it off. It was going to overtake her long before the woodland.

Her weary brain was galvanized to think of a defense. If her pursuer came alongside, caught her rein and pulled her up suddenly she would no doubt fly over Silva's head and that would leave him with the horse as he intended. Her only chance was to forestall him and see if she could get him to fall off by making his horse jink suddenly; then she would have a chance to escape.

She sat hard into Silva and pulled him up as violently as she dared, swinging him around in the same movement. He reared up. She clung desperately to his mane to save herself and saw the chestnut horse skidding toward her. Unable to stop in time, it collided violently with Silva and Minna was knocked flying by its head hitting her painfully in the chest. All the breath left her body and she was hardly aware of her flight through the air, only knowing that this was not what she had intended. Landing with a heavy thump on the rutted track, she was aware of someone rolling beside her and realized that her adversary had been thrown off as well. Stars flashed before her eyes, horror choked her, but she hadn't the strength to move, let alone run away. If this person were to stand up and plunge a dagger in her inert body, so be it: she couldn't defend herself.

But by the swearing and groaning that was issuing from her partner in distress she quickly realized that he was in no fit state to fight her. Turning her head, blinking, she saw a red-haired boy, only – by the look of him – a year or two older than herself. Having expected a hirsute, ugly old brigand, she was so relieved she felt her worst fears receding: this could have been Cerdic or Stuf or even Esca, a callow youth. He was hurt, it was plain, far more than she was, for he seemed unable to get up and was near to sobbing with pain, even though – she could tell – he was trying very hard not to. So Minna allowed herself the luxury of getting back her breath and composure at her leisure. She was no longer the pursued. She had the upper hand now and the relief was euphoric. She sat up and laughed. She pulled out Stuf's evil little knife from its sheath and twisted it in her hands.

"Look, I could kill you now if I wanted."

The boy glared at her. He had the look of a fox cornered by hounds, with his wild dark red hair and furious eyes. He certainly didn't look frightened. He was the sort of boy Minna liked the look of, unlike flat-faced, pasty Esca – but, thank goodness he was disabled, for she would not be happy if their positions were reversed. She thought he would kill her if he had the chance, without hesitation.

"I only wanted your horse," he said. "You didn't think I wanted *you*, surely?" This last spoken with great scorn.

Minna grinned. "You're hurt," she said. "I can't say I'm sorry."

"Thank you for your condolences. I'm touched."

His sarcasm was amusing. Instead of hating him, Minna was now rather drawn to him. He was no longer a threat.

"I could take your horse, as you were planning to take mine. But I won't. I don't want two. I would have killed you if you had stolen mine."

"My father told me to get yours. I've no argument with you. You'd better get on your way – wherever you're going – before my father comes looking."

Minna stood up slowly, her head still spinning a little, and looked for the horses. They were not far away, capering around, enjoying each other's company, bucking and kicking. Even as she watched, she saw Silva stop and put his head down to graze and the other horse, after a few more larks, joined him and started to graze too, obviously as hungry as Silva. Minna knew she would have no trouble in catching Silva again. But her eyes lingered admiringly on his new companion. The horse was as foxy red as his owner, and as handsome too – like Silva, a good cut above the ordinary riding pony found in these parts. He too had some Eastern blood, she guessed, with his fine head and clean legs. He had no white on him at all and his coat was bronzy-dark, like his rider's hair. He made a handsome match with his proud rider. Minna realized she could leave the boy lying and take his horse quite easily. The tables were certainly turned.

But she knew she wouldn't. Another horse now, so near to nightfall, would be a complication too far. And as for the boy…could she leave him? Having spoken glibly of killing him a moment before, she now felt sorry for him, and at the same time despised herself for such weakness.

"What have you done? It can't be that bad."

Or could it? Having helped her mother nurse so many people in the fort, she was knowledgeable about injuries and was pretty sure, after a good look at him, that the boy was suffering a dislocated shoulder. She knew this was extremely painful, but quite easy to mend. Her mother knew how to do the quick wrench to get the joint back in place, but she was not practiced in it and had no intention of trying it out now.

"It's your shoulder?"

He scowled at her, struggling to sit up. His right arm hung uselessly and he clutched it desperately to try and support it. Minna could see that he hated being at such a disadvantage in front of her – a girl! – and was doing his utmost to appear nonchalant and strong, but the pain brought out a sweat on his forehead.

"I'll catch your horse for you, and that's all. He can

take you back. You're lucky I'm not taking him, like you intended to take mine."

The boy was so proud, Minna could see how he hated accepting her help. She liked his spirit: there was a touch of Theo in his arrogant manner. She helped him to his feet and saw that he was thin as a willow stick under his woollen tunic and wolfskin cloak. His skin was brown and dirty but his eyes luminous, almost as dark as Theo's. They were filled with loathing toward her. This pleased Minna. She was the winner!

She caught Silva and the chestnut horse came with her as she went back to the boy. She gave the boy his horse's reins but had no intention of helping him to mount – she needed him to take his time to get back to his camp, else his ugly elders might decide to come looking for her. He would have to walk. There was no way he could mount without help and she wasn't helping him.

"I love your horse. Why do you want mine when you've got one like this yourself?"

"He's my father's, not mine."

"What's his name?"

"Caractacus."

Minna laughed out loud – Caractacus! Caractacus

was the old British king, the son of Cunobelin who these brigands were claiming as their ancestor. They were all crazy! But then she remembered that she had named her horse after a pagan god, Silvanus, so what was the difference? Two fine horses with lofty names.

"And your name? What's your name?"

"Draco."

She might need to know later, although she was not sure why. She had a feeling that they would meet again. She vaulted up onto Silva, her weariness banished momentarily by the euphoria of her success. It was great to show off in front of the vanquished boy. She gathered up her reins and turned the prancing Silva back onto the track. Camulodunum was surely close now and what a story she had to tell Theo!

"Goodbye, Draco!"

"Curse you!" he snarled back.

But Minna didn't hear him as Silva plunged away into his smooth gallop.

Draco stared after the girl with an uncontainable rage rising up inside him. He burst into a sobbing, incoherent tirade of frustration and pain, burying his face in his horse's fine red mane as if to prevent the silent night hearing such agony. To be so humiliated by a *girl*! It was outside his experience – there were no women in his circle: if he had ever had a mother, he knew nothing of her. His father Cintus was everything to him, hard and cruel as he was, and his father's life of pillaging, hiding, killing, suffering, celebrating, feasting, fleeing and hiding again – that was his life too, and all he had ever known. He knew nothing of females, and could not believe that he had been brought down by one of this despised race. And she had laughed! The picture of her bright face as she turned back to mock him was as sharp in his mind as her beastly little dagger might have felt in his heart. He knew she could have killed him if she had wished – a *girl*! It was beyond belief. But it had happened.

The horse fidgeted beside him, wanting home, and Draco let him walk on at last, leaning heavily on his neck. He must find a log or a ditch or something to enable him to climb onto the horse's back, for he would never make it on his own feet. The pain engulfed him, now as strong physically as the pain in his heart, and the tears came, brimming over, mostly now of self-pity. The girl's face danced in his brain.

He would get his revenge on her, he vowed, sobbing. Never would he let a *girl* bring him down like this, and get away laughing! He would find her, wherever she was, on her gorgeous gray horse, and take his revenge. It was only by concentrating on the lovely anticipation of this day that he kept going, stumbling and mumbling through the rutted forest beside his gentle horse.

VII

When Minna came into Camulodunum on her horse she felt like a queen entering her own city. She knew she didn't look like one, but she felt like one. Last night had been terrible, but she had won through. Savoring that triumph gave her such joy that her confidence had come winging back. It was a cold morning but fine at last, the rain cleared away and a bright sun shining out of a cloudless sky. There was no going back: whatever might happen now, Minna was determined to stay in Camulodunum, even if it was to be a mere skivvy in a kitchen somewhere. She was not so optimistic as to think she might be taken into Theo's household, although she knew she must approach him for help. This thought dampened her enthusiasm, for she didn't think he would be thrilled to see her. He had grown out of her, after all. The ruby ring had meant nothing to him. She was the last drop of dew clinging to a flower-bud blossoming in the sunshine. That was how she pictured it.

But Minna was a stubborn and optimistic girl. She was bringing him Silva, wasn't she? How could he turn her away? For Silva belonged to the Roman army and she had stolen him from Othona. Those were the facts and she must face them, however hard.

All the same, she was frightened of facing Theo.

She slipped off Silva's back and led him into the city, not wanting to make herself conspicuous. She came in through the usual hotchpotch of buildings outside the great wall, a tangle of workshops and hovels that straggled along the road and spread into smallholdings and animal pens across the hillside. Many Roman cities had tended to slide into decline in recent years, and the appearance of this one-time capital city was now slightly down-at-heel, although Minna was enough of a country girl to find it awe-inspiring. Brought up in the confines of a small army fort, she was not used to such splendid thoroughfares and huge buildings and such a scurrying of busy people all about their business. She did not notice the trash bins and garbage piled in corners or in deserted buildings, and the unkempt appearance of the huge chariot-racing circus that she passed on her way in; she saw only the splendor and not its fading.

So where would she find Theo? Did he have his own villa or did he live in the barracks? Did he live with Tiberius and Julia? She had no idea. She reached the big square in front of the Temple of Claudius and stopped there and dropped down onto the lower step of the temple, suddenly so tired and confused that she felt she was going to keel over. As if in understanding, Silva dropped his head and nuzzled at her hand. He too was tired and hungry. He did not need to tell her.

"Oh Silva, what shall we do?" Minna whispered.

But as she sat there she heard the distant, unmistakeable slap of army feet marching and saw that the people in the street were drawing back to make way – not to watch, for the people of the garrison town were well used to the army in their streets – just to show respect for authority. It was only Minna who lifted her head eagerly.

She was not disappointed, for it was Theo who led the men. She knew him instantly, even from a distance, from the proud way he held himself, his lithe figure on the mare Pesrut, Silva's dam. Only Theo was mounted. His own bodyguard marched close behind him, and behind them the eighty men who made up the century, along with his second-in-command.

Seeing Theo, Minna's weakness was forgotten. She stood up and only just managed to stop herself from shouting out. But Silva, recognizing Pesrut, flung up his head and whinnied shrilly, with no compunction for etiquette. Theo's head turned and Minna saw the shock go through his body at seeing her. She could not make out from his expression whether the shock was of horror or joy, for his shining helmet hid much of his face, but he made no move to halt – not surprisingly, for a commander was hardly likely to stop his army to talk to a girl. But he had seen her, at least – that was something. Relief and joy bubbled up. Minna hugged Silva with excitement. As the army marched on, Minna saw Theo turn his head and summon one of his bodyguard to come alongside. Theo half-halted Pesrut and muttered something to him, then dismissed the man and rode on, looking forward. Minna stared after him but he did not look for her again, and the army passed by, all in perfect step, and the people started to cross the square again as the sound of marching feet died away.

VIII

Theo laughed. "By all the gods, Minna, I nearly fell off my horse when I saw Silva. What shocks you give me! What are you doing here? Who sent you?"

Theo had come straight from the barracks to the garden of his villa nearby where he now sat with Minna at a table in the courtyard. The sun had decided to shine with a most unusual warmth after so many days of cold rain, and Theo, still sweating from his military exercises in his heavy uniform of leather and metal, had opted for outdoor refreshments. He removed the great burnished helmet and set it on the table. His black hair curled tightly to his head with sweat, and beads of sweat ran down his straight, arrogant nose. Minna sat drinking him in: his glistening golden-dark skin and teasing black eyes...she was so grateful that he was not angry that she could only laugh. She was far from sweating herself, her cloak damp and clammy over her shoulders, but his welcome warmed her like wine. He was pleased, and made no effort to hide his pleasure. That was enough to make up for all the miseries and frights of her journey.

Benoc, serving the food, was not so pleased, she could see, and glowered at her as he set down a dish of baked eggs and cheese with hunks of fresh bread. Minna tried to hold back, to show good manners, but it was all she could do not to fall on the food like a starving wolf.

Theo laughed again. "Go on. I can see you came without provisions. Set to. I'm happy to wait for your explanations."

He ordered Benoc to bring wine and figs and cheese for himself, and helped himself to a piece of Minna's bread.

"You can see I'm not as miserable as I feared I would be. Tiberius has been promoted which makes him happy, so he isn't retiring yet awhile. He has promoted me in turn and has me in training for running a garrison city. That's largely office work, but to keep me sweet he has given me my own cohort. So that makes me happy. The other centurions are all older than me by far but they're pretty slack and my men are starting to show their mettle. My theory is that if we show ourselves to be a cohort well above average I could still be in line for a fighting posting. So it's not as bad as I feared. Not what I wanted, but I'm making the best of it. I have my own villa here beside the barracks, with my own servants – you can see, it's not bad."

The villa was nothing like as elegant as that of Tiberius and his family, which Minna remembered from her brief visit earlier. It was stark and plain, but Theo had never looked for comfort.

He took another piece of her bread and then challenged her: "What's your story, Minna? Why are you here?"

She told him. He wasn't impressed.

"You've run away from marrying Esca? He would have given you security, a home, children – isn't that what girls want? What is there for you here? Perhaps a job in a kitchen or a job as a servant. Is that better? Is that what you want?"

And now his dark eyes challenged her, his words cruelly underlining the true picture. Minna saw at once that he was not going to take her under his cloak as he once had, he was not going to offer her a place in his villa, he was going to shake her off like a burr caught on his tunic in passing.

She lifted her chin.

"I've brought you Silva," she said.

"Yes, I noticed. Silva belongs to the army, you know that. I could have brought him with me without your permission, if I had wished."

"Why didn't you then?" Minna asked angrily.

"Because I didn't want to make you grieve."

Minna fought down a sob. He did care for her! But he was not going to help her. She was totally confused.

Theo saw her state and said kindly, "Come, , we have to be clear about things. You must rest first, and get cleaned up. Benoc will look after you. And after that we'll discuss what's to be done. I'm off to the bathhouse, and then I have to check taxes in kind – we are forever being swindled. But that's natural, I suppose. You see what a civil servant I have become!"

He pushed back his chair and stood up, smiling down at her. The jewels in his splendid leather belt winked in the sunshine and the silver studs threaded into the leather thongs that hung down from the belt jingled as he turned to call for Benoc. To Minna's eyes he seemed to have grown in stature since she last saw him, and certainly in importance. He carried his authority with both swagger and grace: how could she not love him?

Benoc came and reluctantly took her into the austere villa where he made her up a bed in what was a rarely-used guest room. He brought her hot water and towels. He was obviously curious as to what was going on, but as a slave had no right to ask questions, and Minna didn't enlighten him. Perhaps to take his revenge, he turned as he went out of the room and said softly, "Did he tell you he is betrothed to Julia and will marry in the summer?"

He smiled, and padded away, barefooted, back to his quarters.

Minna flung herself on the bed and buried her face in the goose-down pillow. But before the tears could come she fell into a sleep of exhaustion and dreamed not of Theo but of Draco, the boy with the chestnut horse.

IX

"Minna, you don't have to be so cross about everything," Julia complained, turning from her dressing table to watch Minna picking up the clothes she had dropped on the floor. "Theo asked me to give you a job, but I don't find you very good company. Perhaps he should keep you in his own household."

Minna shrank at Julia's words. Spring was coming and the sun was stippling the mosaic floor of Julia's bedroom, the patterns already there further patterned by the shadows of the trees in the garden making a breezy dance over the surface. Minna, in her lowly job of maidservant, was letting her mind wander far from the task at hand, imagining herself galloping beside the sea on her lovely Silva, the fresh smell of ozone and seaweed in her nostrils, the wind in her hair and the lovely warm feel of Silva's sides against her legs. How she longed for her old freedom and the marshes and creeks of Othona! She could not believe her stupid desires, remembering all too clearly how glad she had been to leave. But after several months of working as a maidservant in the tribune's house the lack of freedom was stifling her. Her first overwhelming gratitude at being given a place – engineered, of course, by Theo – was long forgotten and with the coming of spring a wild impatience with her situation was threatening her composure.

"I'm sorry," she said sincerely.

She liked Julia, after all, who was kind enough and treated her more as a friend than a servant. Julia had made her approach a fisherman and send a message back to her mother that she was safe and had a job, something Minna hadn't thought of.

"Perhaps you need a little time to yourself," Julia said. "You've worked hard since you came.

Everyone needs a break, even slaves – not that they get one, of course. But I could spare you for a few days when I go to Londinium with my mother. I won't need you there."

Of course, that was the one outing Minna was looking forward to. She had never been to Londinium. But if she was not to go, the thought of a week to herself was equally attractive.

"Yes, I would like that!" She brightened immediately. Her first thought was whether she would be able to "borrow" Silva, who she still thought of as her own. Theo only rode out for pleasure now, for his command was of an infantry force, and he no longer rode at its head, but walked. Even on the arduous route marches he gave himself no favors, for he had to be as fit, or fitter, than the men he led. The day Minna had met him, he was moving Pesrut to new stables. She had not seen him ride again.

Julia was going to Londinium to buy clothes for her wedding, Minna knew. The wedding was scheduled for the early autumn. It was something Minna refused to think about: it was altogether too painful. But such was her optimism, she had convinced herself that it was never going to happen, mainly because she had never seen Julia and Theo show much affection for each other, although she had seen them together many times. She had never seen Theo kiss Julia, nor noticed that Julia seemed to desire it. Minna had a deep suspicion – incredible as it seemed to her – that Julia's ardor was engaged elsewhere, for she had seen her flirting with a young secretary who worked for her father. From the way the two of them sprang apart at Minna's interruption one day Minna was sure that kisses had been involved. It seemed that the betrothal was much like her betrothal to Esca: an arrangement by the elders, nothing to do with love. Of course it was beyond Minna's comprehension that Julia could prefer the effete young secretary to Theo, but perhaps she did not want to fasten her life to an ambitious soldier who would always put duty to the legion before any domestic considerations. Life with Theo would never be easy. Minna would follow him to the ends of the earth, but Julia would prefer to stay in her comfortable villa with a nice young pen-pusher. Minna had never dared question Theo about the marriage and he had never mentioned it. It did not seem to loom large in his mind.

She saw him when he came to Tiberius's villa,

which was quite often, but had rarely had a chance to talk to him alone.

As soon as Julia departed Minna went to Theo's villa to ask him if she could ride out on Silva. He was at work on army training in the barrack square, but Benoc was sweeping the yard outside the villa and Minna approached him.

"Could you tell him I'm taking Silva? I've got time off."

"Lucky you," was all Benoc could say. Sourly.

Half an hour later Minna had groomed Silva and was on his back heading for the nearest gate out of town. Silva had greeted her with an ecstatic whinny and was now dancing beneath her with excitement at the reunion, anxious for the wild gallop that he guessed was coming. Minna had to hold him up through the crowd by the gate to wait for a big cart of grain, and as she sat waiting she caught sight of a face on the other side of the road that made her catch her breath. It was the boy Draco. There was no mistaking the sharp, ruffianly boy with his dirty tangle of dark red hair, scowling face and tattered clothes. He was watching her with what she recognized quite plainly as hatred, as if not a day had passed since the meeting in which she had so cruelly bested him. The sight of him gave Minna an unpleasant stab of fear. At the same time the vision of his lovely horse came into her mind and she wondered suddenly why she had never suggested to Theo that he should ride out with his bodyguard and look for this exceptional horse. He could easily appropriate it for his own use. The scoundrels who owned him – who had no doubt stolen him – would have no power to stop him. She had assumed that they had traveled on, but here was the boy in Camulodunum, his camp presumably still close by.

Caractacus – that lovely horse! Minna's spirits soared at the thought of capturing him – he was much too good to belong to those brigands instead of to the Roman army. He was a horse to lead a legion, or to carry the standard. If Theo set eyes on him, Minna knew he would want him.

She was so pleased with her new idea that when the grain cart had passed she rode Silva across the road close to the boy, her apprehension quenched. He was no threat to her now that she worked for the tribune's daughter and had the ear of the cohort commander.

"Draco!" she shouted. "Is your arm cured?"

It was good to look down at him from Silva's back.

"No thanks to you, it is. It was nothing," he answered.

Under the dirt he was amazingly handsome. Minna thought of Esca's flat fish-face and laughed.

"Do you still have your lovely horse?"

"My father's horse, yes."

"Who is your father?"

"His name is Cintus. Why are you so nosy? What is it to you, who my father is? Who is yours, as if I cared? Why don't you get on your way?"

He almost spat his words in a broad Celtic tongue; no Roman graces had rubbed off on him, it was obvious. And yet Minna sensed that he was intelligent as well as bold, no mere ignorant brigand, even if that was the life he was living. An instinct told her to be careful; perhaps her cavalier approach was tactless. He made it clear he wanted no friendship, which Minna was disposed to offer, even while she planned to steal his horse. She saw that she was being ridiculous. It was her sudden freedom, gone to her head! She should have passed the boy by, kicked dirt in his face. She tossed her head and pressed Silva on through the gate, confused by her feelings.

Soon she was out on a wide heathland and could

turn Silva's head to the far horizon and let him go. At last she felt the excitement of the wind in her face, the thud of galloping hooves beneath her carrying her at such speed under the blue spring sky – she laughed out loud as Silva's stride lengthened, reveling in the pure delight of knowing this pleasure after so long. She could not remember when she had last felt so happy! Oh Theo, if only you were here with me, she dreamed, even as she laughed! She could not wait to tell him of her great idea.

She longed to see the sea again, but it was too far away. She rode back the way she had first ridden into Camulodunum, past the place where Draco had attacked her, and came onto some rising ground that looked down onto the estuary – as near to the sea as she could get. The day was clear and she could see all the winding, muddy creeks below and the wide river mouth beyond and, far on the other side, the dim splotch that was Othona fort, her old home. The view gave her a twist of homesickness and longing – how strange, for she had no desire to be back there. She missed her mother, and even dour Cerdic her brother, and Stuf. But she was near Theo – that was what mattered.

She took Silva back to Theo's stable and Theo came in while she was still there. He smiled, pleased to see her.

"So, Julia's gone, and you're out to play?"

"She said I could have a day off! I took Silva out – I knew you didn't need him. I told Benoc. You didn't mind?"

"How could I?" He laughed.

"Oh, Theo, listen, I have had such a marvelous idea!"

She told him about Caractacus and how easy it would be to take him. "He is much too good for them. They must have stolen him. They are brigands – I saw them in their camp. They tried to take Silva, so why shouldn't we do the same to them?"

"Perhaps. Where do these people live? Where do we find this magic horse?"

"I don't know. But I could find out. It can't be far away, if that boy Draco was in town. I will find them! If you lend me Silva I can ride out every day and look for them."

"Is that the way a lady's maid spends her day off, gallivanting around the countryside looking for a horse? These gypsies are dangerous people, I think, Minna. I don't like the sound of it."

"Come with me then!"

"Minna, I am on duty all day. Or haven't you noticed?"

"You won't stop me! Oh, Theo, you can't! Please let me ride Silva out! He's doing nothing all day and I have nothing else to do. I just might find where the horse is but I won't approach anybody. I'll keep hidden. Don't say no, *please*! What else can I do all week? I am so tired of being indoors all the time – *please* say I can! Just ride out, I mean—"

She gabbled away and Theo started to laugh.

"How can I stop you? You are a law unto yourself, Minna, and I wouldn't want you changed. But all I say is, be careful. A girl riding alone on a horse as striking as Silva is conspicuous. Don't go near anyone out in the country, keep your own counsel."

But Minna, having Theo's permission, did not think of danger. She was determined to find out where Draco went and find Caractacus again.

X

The weather was fine. Julia sent word that she was staying longer in Londinium and then Minna felt she was in heaven, on vacation, free as air, riding out every day and spending as much time as she dared with Theo. Which in fact was not very much, for Theo worked very long hours. But at least she glimpsed him every day and sometimes shared a meal with him, and he was relaxed with her and amused by her company. She knew better than to abuse his leniency, for she knew he could pull rank very abruptly. She was also aware of Benoc's resentful observation, for he was nearly always in their company, standing with his back to the wall ready to obey Theo's slightest demand. Theo never dismissed him. Minna sensed that he had good reason, but did not dare dwell on the nuances of her relationship with Theo. It was too difficult. She loved him beyond reason, but knew it was unwise to reveal it by word or action. If it showed in her eyes, then to hide that was beyond her.

Sometimes she stayed in his quarters doing jobs to please him which his male servants were not good at: mainly repairing his tunics or making him a new one, or polishing the silverware he rarely used, or planting flowers in his little courtyard. She preferred to be in his quarters rather than in Julia's, where the women servants left at home spent all their time gossiping and quarreling. What on earth they said about her in her absence, Minna did not like to think. But Benoc thawed slightly toward her as she gradually invaded his space. He was younger than all the other servants and Minna realized that he was lonely and – naturally – not enamored of his status. Minna knew that he had come from Rome as a child with Theo's parents and was of a good Roman family, sold by his father into slavery to repay a debt that would have ruined the family. Some father! Minna used to think. Benoc's real name was Valerian. He had been given a Celtic name to demean him. He was intelligent, sharp, and – Minna thought – wasted. But then she thought – so am I! I deserve better than to be a lady's maid!

Dreaming of ways to improve Theo's opinion of her, she found her mind straying back to the subject of the horse Caractacus. She pictured herself riding into the barracks with Caractacus, to present him to Theo. He would be stunned by such a gift. She asked Benoc if he knew Draco. To her surprise he nodded.

"Yes. He lives with his father Cintus down across the river on the old centurion Julius's farm."

"What, he's got an actual home? He lives like a brigand."

"Yes. They're a wild bunch. The place they live – it was the home of Cintus's family way back. Then when Camulodunum became the city which provided retirement homes for Roman veterans – mostly snaffled from the natives, all the best farming land – Cintus's family were turned out and the farm was gifted to Julius's grandfather. So Cintus was raised in a family without land or status, just poor fishermen, and when he grew up and found out about his family history he was so angry he went off and learned to use a sword from an old soldier, and one day he came back and killed all the family in the farm and moved in. That's roughly the story. It's a long time ago now – I suppose it's true. But now he's got a farm and land, he doesn't know what to do with it. He just roams around stealing and hassling Roman settlements – never native places. He's a crazy man."

That explained his son Draco, Minna thought.

"He's got a lovely horse," she said dreamily.

"That's an army horse. He stole it from a dead centurion after a skirmish two or three years back."

"An army horse! Whyever don't they go and get it back?"

"Because they've got more than enough to do around here keeping the peace. Or haven't you noticed? They've bigger fish to fry than Cintus. A large part of the population hate the Romans – there's always trouble somewhere. Unless Cintus does something really serious Theodosius won't bother him."

Having grown up under the wing of the Roman army, her family working for them in the fort at Othona, Minna had never considered the plight of the native Britons whose land and fortunes had been plundered by the arrogant conquerors. But learning that Caractacus was really an army horse made it seem only fair to Minna that he should come back to his rightful place. Now that she knew where Draco lived she decided to do an investigation, unable to rid herself of this wonderful dream where she rode triumphantly into Camulodunum leading Caractacus as a present for Theo.

When she found the farm it seemed as if Fate was conspiring with her to steal Caractacus. He grazed, tightly hobbled, on the hillside behind the derelict farmhouse along with some sheep, two cows and some goats. Save for the animals, the place was deserted. She could easily have ridden down and taken him. It was afternoon, broad daylight, and the only person in sight was an old man shuffling along the lane with a dog, making for the river. Minna slipped down from Silva's back and when the man got close she called out to him. He stopped and looked at her suspiciously.

"Whose farm is this?"

"What's it to you?" He was a Briton, surly and hostile. Minna knew she was too conspicuous on her lovely Silva. It would safer to be roaming on a donkey or rough pony, but Minna was not a girl for caution.

"I'm looking for someone. Who lives here?"

"A man by the name of Cintus. When he's at home, that is, which isn't often."

"He's away at work?"

"If that's what you call it. Thieving and destroying, making a nuisance of himself."

The man was unpleasant, not a one for confidences, Minna decided, and she was glad when he walked on. She could do without his help. She mounted Silva again and took a long look at the farm set on the hillside. It was surrounded by thick belts of woodland. If there was no one at home it would be so simple to slip down the hill, find the horse and hide up in the woods. Was Cintus's reputation so fierce that no one dared steal from him, as he stole – it seemed – from all his neighbors? Minna felt the excitement beating in her bloodstream. Perhaps to come at dusk...hide Caractacus until it was dark...her mind raced.

She studied the farm for three days running and saw no one save a very old woman who once came to the door and threw out some slops.

When she got back Benoc said to her, "Julia is coming home the day after tomorrow. Your jolly jaunts are over, Minna."

"No! Not yet! I need—" She hesitated. What did she need? Courage? Conviction? Should she tell Theo of this great opportunity, rather than dare to take the horse herself? If it went wrong, Theo might send her back to Othona. She agonized, now time was so short. She spilled out her mind to Benoc.

"What shall I do? What do you think? Theo would give his ears for that horse, I know it. And it belongs to the army anyway."

"It's stupid – you, a girl…if you were challenged what could you do? Why not tell Theo about it and he can go and get it. He would still be grateful to you if the horse is as good as you say. You can go with him, show him where it is. Then you will get the credit just the same."

Minna considered this. It was an attractive proposition, riding out with Theo for a little adventure.

"But would he? He's not into pranks like he used to be. He'll say that it's not something a man in his position could consider." She laughed. She knew

Benoc remembered how wild Theo had been once, before the affairs of state weighed him down.

Benoc smiled his cool, sly smile. "I think it might appeal to him. If he goes out of uniform, out of hours. He gets fed up doing all this official stuff. He likes the army, fighting. He hasn't changed at heart. Ask him. You've only got tonight and tomorrow, if Julia's coming back."

The thought of being a lady's maid again after her days of freedom depressed Minna. Like Theo, the affairs of state weighed her down. Remembering that Julia was planning her wedding, that the next few weeks would be all about anticipating her union with Theo, was something Minna found impossible to contemplate.

"Shall I ask him?"

But before Benoc answered, she already knew she would.

"At lunchtime, when he comes in, I will tell him."

"If he's in a good mood," Benoc said.

"Yes."

They both knew he often wasn't.

"I'll do a dish of his favorite figs, with honey. And the best wine," Benoc said.

So when Minna told Theo of her plan and waited while he ate the figs, her heart was racing with anticipation.

"What's so wonderful about this horse that I must steal him?" he asked.

"He used to belong to the army. Cintus's gang stole him. So you will only be bringing him back to where he belongs. If you see him you will want him. He is gorgeous."

"Better than Silva?"

"As good as."

"I'll take a look, if you want. When I've finished tonight, we'll ride out. Our freedom will be over when Julia comes back so we might as well enjoy it."

Did he feel it too – that their lives were ruled by Julia? It was true that he had hardly visited Julia's home and her father Tiberius while she had been away. When Julia was there he had dined with them several times a week, bathing and dressing up after a hard day's work, but since she had been in London he had gone gambling or drinking with garrison friends in the town, or stayed at home working on his accounts or making plans for improvements to the granary stores.

It was May and the evening was long, the sun sinking slowly from a copper-stained sky as if reluctant to leave the quiet sea and the sleepy fields. Woodsmoke curled up from peasants' cooking fires and hung in the breathless sky. They rode out together, Theo on Silva's dam, Pesrut. He wore only a loose tunic – although with his sword in its usual place on his side. As Silva curvetted beneath her, Minna could not believe how happy she was, savoring this outing...if only life could be like this more often! To be so happy made her want to shout out loud with joy, but she contained herself so that Theo wouldn't think her crazy – yet she saw that he was his old laughing self again, like when he was just a boy at Othona and they had fished and swum in the creeks and flushed out deer with their dogs. His now accustomed air of authority was forgotten, and he was happy to canter and gallop although he knew she would outride him on her superior animal. But when he was on Caractacus it would be different!

They came gently to the hill above the farm and pulled up in the lee of one of the woodland belts. The sun, almost gone, threw dark shadows down the hillside and the animals that grazed there laid long-legged patterns across the still bright grass. Caractacus was there, and threw up his head, listening, conscious of their presence. He was still closely hobbled.

"There, look at him. Isn't he lovely?"

Theo had to agree, obviously impressed.

"We've only to help ourselves," Minna said. "There's never anyone here. I've come several times and seen no one."

The old woman didn't count. There was no sign of cooking smoke, no sound.

"He's pretty close to the house."

"The house is empty."

Theo shrugged, very cautious.

Then he said, "You stay here."

He nudged Pesrut forward and she went down the hill. Caractacus put up his head and whinnied. Minna froze at the sound, her heart thumping with apprehension. Caractacus made hobbled, short-jumping steps up the hill to meet Pesrut, and Theo slipped off the mare and went forward with the halter that Minna had given him. He got it over the horse's ears and pulled it tight, then unsheathed his sword to cut the rope hobbles. As he bent down Minna saw a figure bound out of one the outhouses and come running so fast up the hill she scarcely had time to shout a warning. It was Draco.

Theo had freed the hobbles and swung around at Minna's scream. As he did so the chestnut horse made an excited lunge at Pesrut and pulled Theo off his balance and as his back was turned Draco pulled out the sword he always wore and made a wild and furious swing at Theo's legs to disable him.

Theo went down. Minna screamed and raced Silva down the hill. She saw Theo get up, his sword still unsheathed in his hand, and for a moment he faced Draco, who stood in an identical position, sword drawn. Blood poured from a wound in Theo's leg, but it seemed not to affect him as he parried Draco's next wild swing.

Minna had watched Theo's sword-fighting many times in practice and competition, and did not doubt that he would better Draco, but he had rarely faced a partner as insanely furious as Draco, who – it was obvious – was also well-versed in swordsmanship, no doubt by his acclaimed father.

Minna bit her tongue in horror as the sharp clashes of iron disturbed the silence of the dusk. This was the last thing she had envisaged. Whoever came off the worst – and she knew it would be Draco – they would have severe complications on their hands, with either a body or an injured loser to dispose of, as well as the captured horse to cope with. Caractacus was cavorting across the field with Pesrut, his halter dangling, and Minna thought her time would be better spent securing the horses than watching the sword-fight. She could see now that Theo was playing with Draco, but with respect, for the boy was well-trained, and the wound in Theo's leg was hampering him. It was no surface wound but had cut into the muscle. Even if they got Caractacus, Minna could see that her immediate future with Theo was not going to be all joy and congratulation. How happy she had been only a few minutes before! Now all was disaster.

She caught Caractacus and let Pesrut graze, then stood holding the two stallions, watching the fight. Her instinct to be friends with Draco, she could see, was now doomed.

She shouted out, "Can't you stop? Can't we talk about it?"

How feeble! Theo was enjoying himself and Draco's initial wild slashing had matured into intelligent, defensive swordplay. He had been well taught. It could last a long time and was going to end in blood and possibly death, for neither of them wore any protection.

"Theo, stop! It's stupid!"

Theo glanced at her, grinned. Draco's sword flicked up and caught the edge of Theo's tunic, ripping it across, and a bright bloodstain flowered suddenly. Minna screamed. Theo stopped playing and attacked Draco viciously. With a few deft strokes he had Draco tripping backward in the rough grass and a last strike sent Draco's sword flying out of his hand and a long, deep gash opening on his sword arm. Draco fell, shouting with rage, and Theo stood over him angrily, his sword raised.

"No, Theo! No!" Minna screamed. "Don't kill him."

Theo hesitated, then thrust his sword back into its scabbard. He stood staring down at the huddled figure of Draco, then shrugged, turned to Minna and said, "Find those hobbles I cut off. They're in the grass somewhere."

His voice was curt, back to being a commander. Minna scurried, dragging the two horses with her. She brought the frayed ropes back to Theo and he bent down and pulled Draco's arms roughly behind his back and bound his wrists tightly together. He ignored the wound which was bleeding profusely. Draco squirmed and kicked out at Theo's legs viciously and Theo kicked him back hard in the ribs, at which Draco lay quiet.

"A fine evening's entertainment, Minna," Theo said drily. "I thank you."

He straightened up, wincing. Sweat ran down his face and his hair clung damply to his skull. He wiped his arm wearily across his forehead.

"I hope this horse is worth it."

He glanced at Caractacus, whom Minna was finding it hard to keep in order. The two stallions swung and pranced in her hands, while Pesrut grazed quietly down the hill. Minna wanted to see to Theo's wounds but it was impossible. The cut in his leg was deep and bleeding hard, the one on his chest not very serious.

"You need to bind your leg up tightly," she said.

Theo took out his sword again and cut a long swathe off the hem of Draco's tunic. The fabric was filthy and Minna frowned as Theo bound it tightly over the cut, drawing the edges together. It was obvious he wasn't going to bother with Draco's wound.

"If he bleeds to death it'll save us a burden," he said shortly. "We only wanted the horse. Now I've got a wound that's going to keep me laid up for a week and a prisoner who'll be nothing but trouble. Perhaps we should leave him here."

He stared down at Draco, who glowered back at him with furious dark eyes. He was like a cornered wolf, Minna thought, and probably as dangerous.

"But someone taught him to use a sword. You could be useful in the army," he addressed Draco. "Or learn a gladiator's trade. You're wasted living like a derelict. Where's your ambition?"

Draco spat at him. Theo swore and bent and lifted Draco roughly to his feet.

"I don't take slights," he said angrily. "You've chosen. See how you like the prison doors behind you, until you learn some manners. And the wound you've given me – that could be a hanging matter, if I so decide." He said to Minna, "Go and get Pesrut. I'll hold the horses."

Minna handed them over and ran. Everything had gone wrong! Her lovely dream of riding home in the moonlight with the beautiful Caractacus and Theo full of her praises was now all ruined. Theo was angry and in pain and had hardly looked at Caractacus. It only needed Cintus to appear on the scene now and all would be lost.

But the valley was silent and, as dusk drew down, a fresh dew glittered across the grass. Minna felt it between her toes as she came back with Pesrut. Theo lifted Draco bodily and flung him onto the little mare. He put Pesrut's bridle on Caractacus and the halter on Pesrut and mounted Caractacus himself, taking Pesrut's halter.

"I'll see how your fine horse rides, whether it's worth all the trouble you've put us to. I doubt it. But at least it will come back to the army where it belongs."

Minna rode ahead doubtfully. Theo was taking a chance riding the unknown horse, hurt as he was. The horse was not used to a strange rider...what if he bolted? But she could not help turning to look at them and was warmed to see how proudly Caractacus carried Theo: it was as she had foreseen, how well they were matched, each as handsome as the other – *made* for each other. Theo sat so easily on the stallion's bare back and his hand on the reins was relaxed and Caractacus with his high head carriage and arched crest looked like a horse sculptured for a frieze on a great temple. It was the picture Minna had for so long envisaged and as they walked home through the dusk she forgot all the frights and felt warmed and consoled by the sweet glow of success.

A full moon was rising by the time they came to the city gates. The guards leaped to attention when they recognized Theo.

"Take this prisoner and lock him up," he ordered.

They pulled Draco roughly off the mare and hustled him away and Theo rode on to the barrack stables. Minna followed. It was a warm fine night and up the main street lights flared from all the myriad eating houses where people were congregating. Laughter and the babble of voices echoed between the high walls beyond the temple square and children were rolling hoops down the temple steps and chasing stray dogs. It was all so normal, it seemed hard to take in what had happened on the hillside behind them.

The stable hands came to meet them and take the horses, with much murmured admiration of Caractacus.

"Keep him secure. His owner might come looking for him," Theo said as he slipped to the ground. "And the man's famously handy with his sword."

Minna thought this warning was probably well-founded from the stories she had heard concerning Cintus, but it wasn't something she wanted to think about. Nor did she want to think about poor Draco either. As she handed Silva over she was wondering whether she should now go home or whether she dared stay a little while with Theo. He decided for her.

"Go and get Benoc," he said to her.

Having dismounted, he was scarcely able to walk for the gash on his leg.

"And rouse old Princus from the bottle," he ordered one of the grooms. "I shall need his services." Princus was the army surgeon. "Tell him to come to my villa."

Benoc arrived with news for Theo.

"Word has come that Lady Julia is landing here on the high tide tomorrow morning, sir."

A day early! Minna took a sharp breath of surprise and looked to see if Theo's face lit up at the news. But her own gasp was joined by a curse from Theo.

"By Mithras, am I to meet her like this? A fine thing to boast, being disabled by a child! What timing! Get me indoors, Benoc. And you come too, Minna – our games are over now and we'll drink to it before you go back to being a lady's maid. I won't sleep well tonight."

Whether because of his leg or because of Julia's imminent arrival Minna could not tell. But the news of Julia obviously did not lift his heart. Minna rejoiced! If he loved Julia, he would surely be pleased, not angry? She skipped ahead, Theo limping with an arm over Benoc's shoulder. The wound was horrible, gaping wide and still brimming with blood.

"He meant to hamstring you," Benoc said. "At least you've been spared that."

He found an armful of linen to protect the couch as Theo sat down and put his leg up.

"I'll clean it. It needs stitching."

"I've sent for Princus."

"He'll be drunk this time of night."

"Yes. But if he brings his box of tricks you can do it. Your hands don't shake like his. Or Minna here – she's a seamstress by trade."

He laughed at Minna's look of horror.

"Come, Minna – it's not my throat! That boy is very handy with his sword."

"His wound will need treating too," Minna said. "It's worse than yours."

"Yes, but me first," said Theo. "I won, after all. And the horse – the horse, Minna, is probably worth a few drops of blood. It's very nice. You did well tonight."

Resting now, Theo's mood had changed. Minna basked in his congratulation, relieved that he was not angry with her.

The old surgeon came, as drunk as Benoc had predicted. He laid out his tools and Benoc stood over him, hissing his scorn. He guided the trembling hand, muttering oaths. "He's our commander, not an old cow – everyone will see a crooked scar until his dying day. Here, here…"

Benoc's own hand took the needle.

Theo lay back, biting his lip. He looked up at Minna and instinctively she reached out and took his hand. He grasped it hard as the pain stabbed him, but made no sound. The feel of Theo's hand filled Minna with joy, even though it was prompted by his pain. She found the courage to watch Benoc's delicate fingers pulling the flesh together with the fine suture: no wonder Theo valued him as he did, the boy was neat and proficient at everything he was asked to do, and worked for Theo beyond the call of duty. During these last few weeks of freedom Minna had become more friendly with him, and the stand-off once prompted by jealousy had faded. Their love for Theo was no longer competitive. Certainly Minna had no wish to take over the task Benoc was applying himself to now. His stitching was the equal of hers, as fine as any she could apply to a tunic. Old Princus dithered over him, giving orders that Benoc ignored, and when Benoc tied off the last stitch and cut the thread, Princus pushed him aside and poured half a bottle of spirit into the wound, which made Theo sit up sharply and curse him.

"By Mithras, you're a rough practitioner, you old fool. Leave me alone, Benoc can do the dressing. Go down to the prison and do what you can with the young prisoner we brought in. His sword-arm needs to be saved. I count on you to do a good job there. The boy deserves it."

"After he did this to you?" Benoc was surprised.

"I was stealing his horse, wasn't I? Perhaps you should go and see to him too, Benoc. Bandage me up and go with Princus."

After they had gone, Minna was alone with Theo for the first time. He lay on the couch, the lamp beside him turned low. It shone on his face, accentuating the hollows below his fine cheekbones, tracing the line of his straight, arrogant nose and the sweet curve of his lips. Through the open window the soft night breeze brought scents from the garden and the distant echoes of the town's night life. Minna sat beside the small table where Benoc had left wine and water and a plate of sweetmeats. She scarcely dared lift her eyes to Theo's.

"So quiet?" Theo queried.

She looked up. His black eyes were teasing, the old Theo.

"I led you into danger. Look at you now, for Julia. On crutches!"

Theo laughed. "I enjoyed it. The first bit of fun I've had since I've been here. And the horse, Minna – you were right. It's a great ride, as good as Silva. If I get my way and take my army north, to see some fighting, that horse will do me proud."

"I thought you were to be a tame tribune in Camulodunum? That's what Tiberius wanted you for?"

"Yes, but I can see now it's just a waste of my time. I can be a tribune when I'm old, when I've done something in the field. Tiberius promoted me before my time because he wants to retire and give me his job and see Julia married off to someone suitable. It's just to suit him. But I don't want to be wedding fodder. I don't want his job. If he doesn't allow me I shall appeal over his head."

"You don't want to marry Julia?"

"No. And I don't think she wants to marry me. She certainly won't if I go back to being a full-time soldier."

"But what about all these wedding arrangements? All the clothes she's been buying in Londinium?"

"Oh, they love buying clothes, she and her mother. And her mother loves arranging the wedding. But she can easily arrange another bridegroom if she's so enthusiastic about weddings."

"Theo! What will Julia say? You must tell her soon, if you're not going to go through with it."

Minna was shocked by Theo's attitude, and at the same time her heart was soaring with joy. She laughed.

"Marry me, Theo! I'll join the army and march north with you, sew you up when you're wounded, me and Benoc together!"

The words spilled out as a joke, but never were words so heartfelt. She laughed to cover up her feelings and turned away to pour the wine like the good servant she was. She could feel the color flooding her cheeks at her own temerity and dared not look back at Theo.

He said softly, "At least you saved yourself from Esca. What a farce that would have been! Perhaps we should stay as we are, Minna, free to do what we please. Until – if it ever suits us…if time decides…" His voice faded.

Minna's hand trembled as she lifted the wine goblet.

"I don't ask anything," she said. "Only to be where you are."

Theo took the glass, not looking at her.

There was a long silence and then he said softly, "It will pass, Minna. You should have a boy like that one we took prisoner – what spirit! Or Benoc if I were to make him a free man."

"If you go away, perhaps. If there is nothing for me."

"Oh come, Minna. Nothing is going to happen for a while. We should leave these things unsaid. Think of me – untangling myself from Julia, having the wrath of her mother falling on my head, destroying Tiberius's plans, being tied to the city's accounts when I would be leading my army…it's not a pretty future!

And all on crutches, brought low by *a child*! I won't be good company for a few days, I can tell you."

And at that, there was nothing more to say. Benoc returned and Minna went home, savoring the knowledge that there was to be no marriage to Julia.

XI

"Oh, thank the gods!" Julia exclaimed. "I never wanted to marry into the army! What a life! It's all Theo thinks about."

"Well, you've got to marry somebody," her mother rebuked her. "Your father thought he was making you a splendid match. I did too. His parents were such cultured, intelligent people. Whyever didn't they take him back to Rome with them when they went, instead of leaving him in this gods-forsaken country? Now he's just going wild, all that education wasted, wanting to go off fighting – the stupid boy."

Mother and daughter had unpacked everything and Julia's bedroom was awash with gorgeous apparel. Minna had the job of putting it all away tidily in an inadequate number of chests to await – presumably – the next bridegroom.

"I wouldn't mind marrying Probus," Julia said.

"Probus! He's only a scribe! Prayers be to Ceres, we want more for you than that, Julia! You want some riches in your life, don't you?"

"Father could promote him."

Julia's poor mother was furious at the way their plans had been overturned, not unnaturally, and had been in a permanent bad temper since the news had broken. There was no way of forcing Theo, and Tiberius was not much bothered, so she had no one in the family to listen to her woes. Julia was her only child, on whom all her hopes and ambitions were concentrated, and at eighteen the girl should long have been married and bearing children. The fact that Julia was so flippant and unconcerned about her predicament did not help at all.

Minna smiled to herself, having listened to the carry-on ever since Theo and Julia had made public their decision not to marry. In spite of being back to her hated job, she was happy in a way that she had almost forgotten. The great black cloud that had been hanging over her had blown away.

Julia obviously had no regrets. She was enjoying her new purchases, and trying out the new hairstyles she had seen in Londinium. She chattered eagerly to Minna about the wonders of Londinium, the fine buildings and commerce on the river, and the fashionable people.

"Poor old Camulodunum has had its day, even if it was the first Roman capital. Now it's all down there, Minna – you should see the shipping, and the great forum, and the entertainment in the amphitheater! It was wonderful. Although everyone says it's not the city it was. They all say Rome is going downhill since Constantine died…the good times are over, doom and disaster are on their way. They talk like that around the dinner tables, just as they do up here. They get the news from Rome much sooner than we do so perhaps they're right. It didn't feel like it though. I thought it was all wonderful."

Minna thought of riding dear Silva every day over the rolling country, the glint of sea in the distance, the wind in her hair, and would not have changed her time off for Julia's, for all Julia's prattle of the wonders of Londinium. It was hard coming back to the life of a servant. She was not, officially, a slave, but might just as well have been. Sent on an errand to buy some sewing thread to match a silken scarf that Julia tossed her, Minna met Benoc in the market and asked him the question that was in her mind.

"How is Draco? Is his arm mended? What is Theo going to do with him?"

"Yes, his arm is improving. No thanks to Princus, I might add, more thanks to me. I have been visiting him every day. Theo doesn't know what to do with him. He thinks he's too dangerous to let loose."

Minna laughed.

"I would like to see him."

"Leave him alone! It would humiliate him, to have you see him in prison. He is like a wildcat. Theo thinks he will go crazy if he is held much longer. He makes me give him an infusion of valerian root to calm him down, make him sleepy. But he won't drink it. He spits it all over me."

Benoc grinned.

Minna guessed they were a well-matched couple, Draco and Benoc. They should be friends, not enemies.

*   *   *

It was true that Theo was worried about Draco. He visited him a few times in the evenings, when he was free. He took a flask of wine with him and when the guard had locked the door behind him, he offered the flask to Draco. Draco knocked it out of his hand. Theo caught it before it fell, and took a swig himself.

"Suit yourself."

He sat down on the bare bench that was Draco's bed. The prison cell had a tiny window high in one wall through which a last ray of sun slanted across the ceiling like the reflection on a sword blade. It did nothing to combat the dampness that gleamed on the slimy walls and little to lighten the depressing dark. Theo knew why Draco's misery was so uncontainable.

"If I free you, what would you do?" he asked.

"I would get my father to come and kill you," Draco muttered.

"Exactly. Which is why I won't. Is it your father who taught you to use your sword?"

"Yes. My father is the best swordsman in all of Britain."

"So I've heard. It's a pity he doesn't put his skill

to better use. I would free you if you agreed to my conditions."

"Which are?"

"To join the Roman army and improve your swordplay. To rise up in the ranks quickly, as I know you would, and take command. To take pride in yourself, your person, to fight for a proper cause."

Draco was silent.

"To take care of your horse again," Theo said.

Draco's eyes flickered. He stood against the wall, as far from Theo as he could get, a proud but beaten figure, gaunt with refusing the food that was offered. He had been cleaned up, his hair cropped, a decent tunic supplied. His arm was still heavily bandaged, but Theo knew it was not infected. He would live to ply his sword another day.

"You could train to be a gladiator, that's a possibility."

"Gladiators get killed."

"The best ones don't. They get rich and famous. And you would be the best. And you could kill Romans, which would suit you, and get cheered for it."

Theo took another few swallows of wine.

"I'd rather you become a soldier. You are brave and

clever, exactly what the army wants. You are wasted, living like a derelict. What future is there for you if you stay with your father?"

"My father would kill me if I joined the Roman army."

"Your father is too fond of killing, from what I hear. He cares nothing for you, the way he lets you run wild. What has he gained by spreading fear and distress to innocent people who have done nothing to harm him? He is living in the past. What is the point of that? I am offering you a future, a fine future. I know you are a cut above my ordinary recruits and I want you to take this opportunity."

Draco did not reply.

Theo offered the wine flask again. "Here. Be friends. I care about you."

This time Draco took it, although reluctantly.

Theo got up from the bench. "Think about it. You won't get out of here otherwise."

He signaled to the guard through the bars to unlock the door. "I will call back," he said curtly, and went out.

XII

Three weeks later Minna was sent out to buy some seeds for Julia's private garden and was browsing through the marketplace when an unkempt youth blundered into her.

"Just keep walking," he said, "or you'll die."

She looked down and saw he had a dagger in his hand. She stopped, more puzzled than afraid, but then another man closed in on her other side and clamped a heavy hand on her shoulder.

"Get moving, and keep quiet." Such was his authority that Minna obeyed him. The dagger pricked her painfully, quickly, in her thigh, and drew blood through the stuff of her tunic. She gasped and the dirty youth took her by the elbow and steered her through the crowd. The two of them pressed her close and walked fast. Minna looked around frantically for someone she knew, but no one was interested. What was happening to her? Now she was truly frightened.

They came down past the temple toward the river gate. Now the men had her in a hard grip by the wrists, one on each side, and she had lost her chance of escaping. She could see the barrack walls and the gates into the courtyard of Theo's villa, but there was no one she knew to be seen. The road was busy as usual with laborers and market people, but they were not the sort of people who would help her if she shouted out to them: her guardians were too brutish to accost. She guessed they were Cintus's men. Who else was her enemy? Was she to be held for ransom in exchange for Draco? Or perhaps she would be killed. Cintus had a cruel reputation. What a morass she had dragged poor Theo into, with her innocent plan to take the lovely horse! Only he could save her now, and how he would curse! Cintus was cunning and would kill Theo if he could. Her mind teemed with possibilities, but they were all disastrous. She would have wept if she were not so proud.

Once through the gate the men took a rough path away from the main way and when they were clear of people they took a cord and tied her hands tightly behind her back. Just as Theo had disabled Draco with the horse's hobbles, now she was as hopelessly impotent, stumbling off-balance along an overgrown path through deep woodland. The dagger was still in evidence, and the two youths were laughing with their victory, mocking her with their rough native voices. She could hardly understand what they said. No Roman culture had rubbed off here, that was evident. These men were scum, and she was in their power.

She guessed that the way was a shortcut to the farmhouse where Caractacus had grazed, and was proven right when they came out of the woods at the top of the long hill above the farmhouse. From this point it was still as sweet a view in the summer sunshine as one could wish for, with the glint of the river winding beyond and the far silver streak of the sea horizon glittering under a cloudless sky – its beauty twisted her as she stumbled down the slope. This might be the last time she was to set eyes on the fair earth for all she knew. Tears blinded her and she knew now that she was deeply, horribly afraid. And for Theo too.

The men manhandled her into the farmyard and shouted through the open door. An answering roar came from inside.

So now she was to meet the famed Cintus.

She had expected a larger version of Draco, but how much larger she was unprepared for. The man was huge, a bear, yet not fat. The impression of power and ferocity was every bit as forceful as she had been led to believe. He was as filthy as the rest of them, with the same bedraggled, knotted hair and tattered leather clothes. He had been handsome once, perhaps as handsome as Draco, but now his face was pockmarked and scarred, his nose reddened and bulbous with drink. But he moved like a boy, active and quick in spite of his bulk, the famed sword swinging at his side.

He came up close to Minna and stared at her with manic, reddish eyes. She could smell his foul breath, and stepped back in distaste.

"This is the right one? You are sure?"

"Theodosius's minx, yes."

Minna screamed at the insult and kicked out at the speaker, catching him hard below the shin bone so that he staggered. He hit her across the face. She tried to bite him, but was wrestled into subjection.

"A little she-cat!" Cintus was laughing. "She has spirit! Worth fighting for – I hope the commander will agree."

"He will come and wipe you out. The whole Roman army will destroy you," Minna spat at him.

"The whole Roman army will come to a standstill if I stand before them with you as my shield, and my sword at your throat. Think of that, my little child. Will your commander allow you to be killed? Shall we put him to the test? Perhaps he doesn't care for you that much, after all. We shall find out."

Another younger man came out of the farmhouse, not quite so dirty and rather like Draco in appearance. Minna guessed he was a brother. Cintus turned to him.

"You can take the message, now we have the girl. Speak to the commander in person, to no one else. Go to his villa and wait for him if necessary. You know what to say."

"Yes."

"If you don't come back, the girl will be killed. Make sure he knows that. Within twenty-four hours."

The man nodded and set off at once, but not hurrying.

They shut Minna in a windowless storeroom with huge bars across the outside doors. It was pitch-dark and the only sound was the scurrying of rats in the grain.

XIII

"My master Cintus has taken the girl Minna and will kill her unless you bring Draco back to him. You must come unarmed and alone, save for Draco. If you bring your guard, she will be killed before they reach us."

The words went around and around in Theo's head. Whyever had he not foreseen this event? It was so obvious: the stealing of Minna to exchange for Draco. So simple. Cintus was a genius. But everyone knew he was not to be trusted.

Theo had not received the message until the evening, when Benoc told him, in some dismay, that there was a filthy man waiting to speak to him. He also said that Julia had sent word inquiring for Minna. She had gone to market in the morning and not come back. It was now nearly dusk and they were very worried. Theo had immediately linked this disappearance to the stranger waiting to speak with him, and was not surprised when he received the ultimatum.

"Tell Cintus I will send a reply in the morning. If a hair of the girl's head is harmed, the army will seek you out wherever you are and kill you all."

The man smirked. "It is not army business. It is personal."

"Perhaps." How personal? That was the rub. Theo knew he would put his life on the line to save Minna. The thought of her in the hands of those barbarians sickened him. If they defiled her, he would kill Draco in front of them. His anger surged when the man had departed and, without waiting for his supper or changing out of uniform, he stormed off to Tiberius's villa. He found him in the atrium with his wife and Julia, just about to go into dinner.

"Well, you have to give it to Cintus – what a clever devil he is," Tiberius said placatingly when he heard the news. "We will wipe him out. He has caused too much trouble for too long."

"But our hands are tied while he holds Minna."

"Minna is of little account," Tiberius said.

"Oh, Father, how can you say that!" Julia shrieked at him. "You would let her be killed?"

"Really, no, Tibby!" twittered his wife. "That's too cruel! You can't—"

"By Jove, she is of no account when this tyrant is at our disposal! He is putting himself in our hands. Waiting for us. Of course we must take our chance."

"Ask Theo if he will," Julia shouted at him. "If you command him, he will refuse."

"I think not. He is in no position to refuse," Tiberius said quietly.

"He isn't only a soldier. He's flesh and blood, or haven't you noticed?" Julia shrieked. "Do you not see what is right under your nose – Theo and Minna? Don't you—"

"Julia, hold your tongue!" her mother snapped.

"I think Theo must eat with us and I can discuss the situation with him without input from two hysterical women," Tiberius said coldly.

Theo was horrified by the direction the conversation

had taken, and cursed himself for coming so intemperately to Tiberius. Of course Minna was of no account to the legate – whyever had he thought differently?

"I have not bathed or dressed," he excused himself. "I will come to you first thing in the morning, sir, and we can talk alone. But I thought you should know the situation. It has to be resolved quickly."

"Very well. We'll discuss it then. But you will do nothing until you get your orders from me."

Theo cursed himself as he left the villa. Was Julia going to spend the dinner time explaining to Tiberius that his right-hand man had refused his daughter in preference to a servant? That was not going to advance his ambition. It was almost dark now and he thought sadly of Minna in the hands of what he thought of as barbarians. She must be terrified. She must also be convinced that he would save her. She put such faith in him. There was no way he could concur with Tiberius's idea of a frontal assault with the army.

He got back to his villa and shouted for Benoc to attend to him in the bathhouse. As he lay on the hot slab with Benoc massaging his shoulders (the feel of it always made him want to purr like a cat) he found himself relaxing, seeing in truth what he had to do. He would not go back to Tiberius for orders. He would go to Cintus as directed and if he was killed, so be it. But he knew he was as clever as Cintus. Just as Cintus held Minna, so he held Draco. If he could not make good with such an ace in his hand, he deserved to die.

"You will come with me," he said to Benoc. "So that one of us, at least, will go home to tell the tale."

"Will you go unarmed, as he asked?"

"Without my sword? I shall feel naked."

"You can lay it down, if he wants to parley. Or I can hold it. You cannot be without it, meeting Cintus. He is not to be trusted."

"No. He's a devil. We'll go at first light, Benoc, and with luck be back in time for my day's work. If, as he suggests, we merely exchange prisoners, it will take no time at all."

"I don't think it will be as simple as that."

"No, I think that too."

Minna cursed herself for being stupid not to have foreseen the situation she was now in.

She had not been flung into the farmhouse to be picked over by the oafs that now seemed to be living there, but locked up for some specific reason – no doubt, to be used as a lever in some bargaining process to get Draco back. Cintus had barked in no uncertain terms to the men who had wanted to rough her up: "Don't touch her! She's not a plaything. She's a hostage."

Julia always had her bodyguards with her – she would have been a better hostage, but not easily taken. Minna knew her own value was slight as far as Tiberius was concerned, but Theo…? How much did she mean to him? Surely he would rescue her? Or was it up to her own ingenuity to get her out of this predicament?

But she quickly saw that the last alternative was hopeless. She was locked in an extremely strongly-built shed – surprising from the appearance of shambles that the homestead gave. In the faint light that filtered in through a narrow opening high in the wall – too narrow to wiggle through even should she manage to reach it – she could see no way of getting out. Heavy bars had clunked into place outside to hold the door fast shut and a quick exploration showed no chance of burrowing under the foundations, nor finding a way out by the roof. She was quite helpless. By the gods, what a fool she had been not to have foreseen her vulnerability.

She slumped down with her back against the stout planks.

"Oh Theo, I want you! I need you!"

How soon would he find out what had happened? Not until Julia found her missing in the evening – even then would Theo be told? But they would look for her at his villa, surely, and then... Her life was completely in his hands.

There was no one to see her so she wept with self-pity, giving way to racking sobs of fear and frustration. What was the point of being brave when there was no one to impress? But after the first wild outburst of despair she felt better, her courage returning. A sliver of optimism returned. Theo would never let her die, would he? Would he? Draco could go and Cintus would surely free her. Her head went around, chasing the possibilities. But Theo had to do what Tiberius ordered, and Tiberius didn't care a toss for his maidservant's life. Why should he? Slaves were put to death for trivial misdemeanors, kicked for a sour look. But Theo loved her, didn't he? All questions with no answers. She cried out Theo's name aloud, racked with her love for him. But there was nothing she could do. By her own carelessness she had put a terrible dilemma on him. What a fool she was!

She had no respite from her grief and frustration. No one came. No one brought her food or drink, or brought her a blanket when the cold night air seeped into the hut. The floor was bare earth and the place was empty save for a load of firewood and heaps of rotting grain. As night came the grain started to rustle to the movement of rats. Minna moved to the farthest corner and crouched, shivering, against the wall. From the woods a distant owl cried for its mate and faintly came the echo of a fox barking for his vixen, and she in her prison cried for her love and the unhappy state she was in, and dread for what tomorrow would bring.

Who slept that night? Not Minna, nor Theo, who lay staring into the darkness trying to work out the probable turn of events in the morning. Cintus was a cunning devil. Theo tried to read his mind, determine what he would do if he were Cintus. He would want Draco first, but he would also want the man who had taken him. Cintus did not like to be bettered. Theo knew he had bettered Cintus and would likely pay the price. He cursed himself that he had not foreseen the simple device whereby Cintus had gotten him cornered.

He slept in snatches, suffered nightmares, and called for Benoc to light the lamps. He prayed. He called on all the gods he knew, prostrating himself before the villa's shrine to Mithras; then remembered he was a Christian, and prayed to the one and only God. In his heart he preferred the old gods of war, but Christianity was now the official religion. Did the gods care? He had never seen much evidence of it, but many men had died for Christianity, so perhaps it had some might. In the darkest hour of the night he thought he was unlikely to return from his visit to Cintus, but he told himself he had chosen a soldier's life and to experience this fear was good training. It was how it must feel to face battle, waiting in the long hours of the night for dawn to break. In his past experience everything had happened so quickly there had been no time to feel fear, only excitement. So call this training, he convinced himself. But this time there was only himself, there was no army behind him.

He had never felt so alone. But never for a moment did it occur to him not to go to Minna's aid. It did not even cross his mind.

The night was short and at the first glimmer of light he got up and dressed.

"Go and warn the guard I want Draco. And the horse Caractacus. And pray they will return with us, dear Benoc."

He smiled and laid his hand on the boy's shoulder, seeing that Benoc was biting his lip and trying not to show his fear.

"Don't be afraid, Benoc. They won't trouble with you. They said I am to go alone but you are only a slave and don't count. They are on the side of slaves. It's only Roman pigs like me they're after. But remember, above all, Minna must not be harmed. Whatever happens…"

Perhaps he was doing everything wrong: not to take even an unarmed soldier to guard Draco, only the slender, effeminate-looking Benoc.

"But I want my sword," he said. "I will lay it down when I meet Cintus, but it must be at hand."

"You want your cuirass, at least?"

"No. Nothing. No helmet. And you, Benoc, put your dagger in your belt."

The surprised guard brought Draco out, a man on either side of him, and a groom brought Caractacus, still with straw in his tail.

Theo had Draco's arms bound tightly, and ordered the horse's tail brushed. The men were half-asleep and astonished at their orders, but asked no questions. Theo mounted Caractacus and got Draco hoisted up in front of him.

"You'll have to walk, Benoc, but hold my saddle. We'll not go fast for we need the light of day for our parley."

"Where are we going?" Draco asked.

"To your father."

He nudged Caractacus with his heels. The horse wheeled eagerly and pranced across the cobbles. Theo held him in, smiling.

"Minna was right about your horse, Draco. I won't give him up easily."

"And me? You're taking me back?"

"Yes."

"You're a brave man to face my father."

"I have you to bargain with. It could be that you have to be brave, too, Draco, if your father tricks me. If he tricks me I will kill you."

He felt a shiver go through Draco.

"My father will kill you first!"

"I trust not."

Theo was thinking he had started out too early, the sky showing only a cold, mother-of-pearl gleam to seaward, the river shrouded still in mist. He made Caractacus walk slowly. The horse's legs made a long trail through the wet spring grass as he made his way across the common grazing land toward the woods. In the early summer morning the world was as beautiful as Theo had ever seen it. Because he was acutely aware that it could well be his last he drank it in painfully, not a man usually to notice much about nature, save to study it as an aid to marking out an advantageous battleground. He heard the cuckoo calling from far away, answered by another near at hand and saw a pair of foxes slinking through a ditch. Through a gap in the trees ahead he had a glimpse of the river snaking beneath a canopy of mist toward the sea and, high above, the fingernail of a new moon fading before the spreading light. The morning was completely still; not a breath of wind stirred the archway of the oak trees that their way passed under. The bright leaves spread immobile, gleaming with dew. They passed through the silent woodland and came out on the brow of the hill above the farmhouse. The valley lay before them, still and steaming faintly in the first light of the sun. Cobwebs flung a glittering filigree across the grass. Theo pulled up.

He felt Draco shiver against him.

"Does your father rise early?" Theo asked. "I want this business over and done with."

"If you shout, someone will come out. There's always a lookout."

Even as he said this a figure appeared in the doorway of the house. Caractacus put up his head and whinnied, and another horse answered him from inside a building. The man looked up, startled, and saw them.

Theo slipped off the horse and pulled Draco down after him. He said to Benoc, "Take the horse into the trees and tie him up."

He stood waiting, grasping Draco firmly by the arm.

"No tricks from you, Draco. I don't want you dead any more than your father does. But you will surely die if your father doesn't give me back the girl."

Draco was white. Theo suspected that he did not

trust his father any more than he did. Benoc came back.

"Take my sword off me," Theo ordered him.

Benoc unbuckled the jeweled belt and took the sword.

"Follow me, not too close. But bring the sword."

He started down the hill, walking slowly. As he did so, Cintus himself came out of the house. Theo halted and stood holding Draco. Cintus could see he was unarmed.

"Bring the girl," Theo shouted.

Cintus stared with his narrow, piggy eyes and gave an order. Several men had now appeared out of the farmhouse. One of them went back in and in a few moments came back holding Minna. She came bedraggled, saw Theo, and screamed his name. Her whole mien changed at the sight of him, as if a charge of power galvanized her. Her head came up: color flooded her cheeks and her eyes sparked with defiance and confidence.

"Theo!"

But after the first rush of relief at seeing her unharmed, Theo's eyes went back to Cintus. He too was unarmed, unless he hid a dagger in his filthy rags.

But was it going to be this easy, to exchange the two youngsters and depart? The two men faced each other, still some thirty meters apart. Holding Draco, Theo could feel the boy's trembling anticipation.

"Bring him here," Cintus ordered.

"Bring Minna," Theo countered.

Cintus jerked his head and the man holding Minna came up the hill toward them. Theo went to meet him. Draco and Minna stood side by side with their guardians, and Cintus stood apart.

Theo waited. He had no idea what Cintus was up to. But as far as he could see none of them were armed.

Then Cintus said, "I think we will fight for them. You and me. The winner takes both."

And he laughed, a croak of a laugh, showing disgusting black teeth. He turned to his motley band of companions and shouted, "What do you say, boys? A bit of fun, eh?"

They put up a ragged affirmation, while Theo tried to take in the enormity of the man's proposition. He was to fight to the death for Minna, while Cintus would do the same for his son. He saw at once that Cintus's confidence was such that he knew he would win, take Minna, take his son back, and bring down the commander of the Roman cohort all in one fell swoop. A victory indeed!

Cintus waited, grinning, for his answer.

Theo tried to think of a way out and couldn't. But the challenge was not complete anathema to him. The man underestimated his opponent's skill for a start. Theo did not know of anyone to date who could overcome him, save for a few of the trained gladiators who had taught him. Perhaps he had not gotten as much practice in since coming to Camulodunum, but he thought he was fitter than Cintus and certainly younger.

"Get your sword then. We shall fight."

Benoc came forward with his sword. Theo said softly to him, "If it goes wrong, Benoc, forgive me."

The look on Benoc's face was heart-rending. Theo did not dare look at Minna, but Draco muttered to him, "You are going to get killed. I am sorry."

"Really? If I win, will you come back with me and be a good soldier?"

"Yes."

This, strangely, put heart into Theo. He was not averse to this contest, even though it was so dangerous.

He was a solider, after all. It was something that happened to soldiers, hand-to-hand fighting. It was a part of life. And death.

He looked around him while Cintus waited for his sword to be delivered, and took in the beauty of the scene, the tranquility of the fields where the long shadows of morning stalked, the distant calling of the cuckoos in the woods. He was filled with resolution, and remembered his parents in Rome. His father, after all, had trained him for this.

He lifted his sword and sliced through Draco's bonds. The cords fell on the ground. Draco stayed where he was, rubbing his arms.

"If it comes to it, Draco, I trust you to protect Minna," Theo said, very softly.

"Yes."

Cintus saw how close he was to Draco with the sword in his hand, but made no move. He shouted something to the man guarding Minna and the man picked up the cut rope and tied one of Minna's wrists to Draco's.

"A fine pair," Cintus shouted. "Two for the price of one! How's that?"

He laughed uproariously, and took his sword

from the man who brought it. It was a fine sword, Theo could see, not pirate garbage. Cintus swished it through the air happily.

"Come!" he shouted at Theo. "Show me your mettle."

Theo thought to himself: When I kill him he will have a look of great surprise on his face. He doesn't respect me.

And that knowledge gave him a great stiffening of courage. This was beyond anything that had happened to him before and his mind was now totally concentrated. He saw nothing but the sword before him, clutched in a hand as large and knife-scarred as a soldier's platter. He was back in the training-ground with the head of the gladiators, who knew more than Cintus would know in a lifetime. And much of it he had taught Theo. Enough.

XIV

Minna could not believe this dreadful thing was happening. And she knew the situation was entirely of her own making. It was she and she alone who had delivered Theo into this impasse.

He stood in the dawn sunlight, his sword in his hand, completely unprotected in just a simple tunic. Cintus was so covered in old scraps of skin and fur he could well have been wearing a cuirass beneath. He looked scarcely human, Minna thought, like some old bear out of the forest, yet for all his bulk he was extraordinarily light on his feet. By contrast

Theo looked a boy, so slender and lithe, but Minna knew his body was as hard and fit as Roman training demanded. They were circling each other, looking for the first opportunity, and Minna knew that if they were evenly matched this fight could take a long time and likely be as punishing to the winner as to the loser. In some fights both died, even when one was the winner. She had never seen a real gladiatorial contest, but had heard a lot about them, and this was in essence the same.

Draco said bitterly, "You did yourself no favors, stealing our horse."

Minna was too proud to agree, but knew it was true. Being tied to Draco was a penance; she hated him, although he had all the qualities she admired. *"Two for the price of one!"* Dear gods, if Cintus won her life would not be worth living! She would kill herself, and join Theo in the afterlife.

The clash of steel rang out suddenly in the quiet morning, the first parry initiated, so quick that Minna could not see who spied the opening, and then the sun flashed off the blades as they swung in an intricate dance, up and around and down and across until there was a stoppage, body against body, the great weight of Cintus causing Theo to step back, disengage, and come again so quickly that Minna could not follow. But she saw a quick spurt of blood somewhere among the tatters of a ragged sleeve and heard Cintus bellow, and his rage galvanized him to make furious killing thrusts that Theo had to dodge or die. This was rough peasant fighting which Theo scorned and, after dancing backward to let Cintus take heart, he stopped him with a vicious upward cut that nearly knocked the sword out of Cintus's hand, so violent was the meeting of steel on steel. Minna saw sparks fly and shuddered. Cintus roared and spun with the impact, and Theo followed up with a brisk cut which would have had Cintus's head off if he hadn't ducked in time. As it was some of his tangled locks flew off like dandelion seed in the breeze.

Minna let out her breath in a gasp of relief. She felt Draco shudder beside her. They were as one in their hypnotized concentration and Minna felt that something in their natures was being bound together just as their arms were bound, by living through this unbearable contest together.

But then Draco said, "I don't want your commander to die."

"I thought you hated us all!"

"His life is more valuable than my father's."

Minna was amazed. "Tell your father that. Shout to him!"

But she knew he wouldn't. He couldn't. They could only wait. The gods would choose whose life to preserve.

There was to be no quick victory. Cintus's rough crew brought out ale and sat in the grass drinking and talking while the two contestants fought and Minna's concentration faltered, unable to follow the pattern of the fierce climaxes, feints and tricks and the few almost friendly withdrawals to get back breath and strength which then renewed the ferocity of the attack. The great weight of Cintus's body, she could see, could easily split Theo in two halves if he let himself get in the way, but Cintus was at the mercy of Theo's lightning reactions. Their style of fighting was very different and each was beginning to fathom the other's possible weakness, easier for Theo than for Cintus. Cintus had had no classical training but his practice over many years in bloody infighting was far more than Theo's, and he had tricks that were not in Theo's book and which Theo would not stoop to.

He was a very dangerous opponent.

It was as if act one of the performance had taken place and now a more serious appraisal was starting. Each was looking for the fatal opening, and trying to tempt the other to make the wrong move and reveal it. Theo was too experienced to fall for Cintus's crude feints but the defensive fighting became long drawn-out and Minna could see that both fighters were beginning to tire. Their prancing shadows were now shorter over the churned turf and the heat of the sun was making itself felt. Sweat trickled down the rapt faces.

Suddenly Theo, having backed off as if to take a breather, sprang forward with a fine thrust that was missed by Cintus's wild parry. But as he parried Cintus sidestepped and the thrust that would have killed him went under his arm. Cintus bawled out with rage as a bright spring of blood flowered among the rags of his sleeve; Theo stepped back and a wild swing of retribution from Cintus caught him even as he jumped aside, a skimming cut that caught the top of his shoulder and sliced into his muscle. Neither cuts were on the sword-arm but both were serious enough to weaken from the flow of blood.

Minna thought at this stage that perhaps the two men would show respect for the other's courage and draw back, concede and shake hands, but now it became clear that this was a fight to the death as intended, and no quarter was to be given. As the two men tired, their swordplay became more erratic and their defense slower, and soon they were both bleeding freely from several scores after tussling, indecisive skirmishes. Theo had a cut that had nearly taken out his eye and the flow of blood was half-blinding him, and Cintus was badly hampered by a cut on the side of his neck which stopped him from turning his head freely.

Minna felt a compulsion to shout at them to stop – the fight was now savage and disgusting. It was at the stage where, in the amphitheater, the crowd would start baying like dogs for the final, fatal blow, when the fighters were too disabled to demonstrate their skill. She had lost all sense of time. The sun was now well up, all the cobwebs long gone and the men of Cintus's gang had run out of ale and were standing around, chatting in low voices, their eyes never leaving the fighters. Benoc was standing like a statue, white-faced, clutching Theo's sword-belt to his chest. What would he do without Theo? Minna wondered. He would be a free man, but with no point to his freedom. What would she do without Theo? She would die.

She shut her eyes. It was unbearable.

Then suddenly there was a scream. The men shouted. They were running. Draco was dragging her by their bonds across the grass. The two fighters were lying side by side, Theo curled up as if asleep, Cintus on his back, a great snoring, rattling noise coming from him. His sword was lying on the grass, red with Theo's blood, but Theo's sword was sticking upright out of the big man's chest, its jeweled hilt even now twinkling in the sun's rays, emerald and ruby and sapphire. How beautiful it was!

Minna screamed. Cintus's men converged on their fallen leader and one reached for Theo's sword to pull it out. They would kill Theo even now!

"No! No!" she screamed.

But Draco dragged her to the side of his father's body and reached for his father's sword in the grass. He then turned on the man wrestling with Theo's sword in Cintus's chest and with his father's sword upraised would have sliced off the man's hand if the man had not jumped back.

"Leave my father! Get back, get back to the farm, all of you! There is no place for you here! Get away! Get away!"

He was like a madman, swinging the sword, straddling his father's body. Minna lurched helplessly beside him.

"Cut me off, Draco! Let me go!"

But the dagger slicing the cords was Benoc's, his white face close to her own.

"Praise be to the gods, Minna. See to the master, help me!"

Released, Minna fell to her knees beside Theo, Benoc beside her.

"Theo! Theo!" she sobbed.

But his eyes were open, coal-dark, brimming with triumph, his lips smiling.

"I got the devil!"

Blood poured down from a gaping cut over his forehead and his wet hair was full of blood. His tunic was all cut up and flowered with blood; even the old wound in his leg had opened up as if in sympathy and seeped into the cold grass. But he sat up, twisted over and then kneeled down and kissed the grass and words of thanks to his gods fell from his lips.

Benoc and Minna were moved to join in and add some words of their own, as heartfelt a prayer, Minna thought, as had ever passed her lips. Then they were helping Theo to his feet and he stood, shaking, looking down at the now still and silent body of his adversary. Draco still stood over him, holding his father's sword. Tears ran down his cheeks.

Theo stepped forward and put his arm around the boy's shoulders.

"Forgive me, Draco, but I had no choice."

He pulled his sword free from the body and handed it to Benoc, then turned back to Draco.

"There is a place for you in my guard, if you want it – a proper life, Draco. Come back with us. Not to prison, to my house. I will send some men down to give your father a proper burial."

Draco made no reply. Minna could see that it was not something to decide in a moment, but she could see that there was no time for Theo to stand around chatting. His body was trembling and he only stood by a considerable effort.

Benoc said to her, "The horse Caractacus is tied up in the woods there. Go and get him, we need him here."

She ran. She could not believe how wonderful, suddenly, the morning was, how beautiful the sun, how loud the singing of the birds, how wild the happiness in her running. She was free! Theo was the victor! She shouted thanks to the gods and the horse Caractacus heard her coming and whinnied and she shouted to him: "Caractacus, you are so beautiful!" The cause of all her horrors! But in the sunlight his coat shone like polished copper and his bold eyes asked for freedom: he was so glorious, fit for an emperor. Fit for Theo. She vaulted, spring-heeled, onto his back and galloped back down the hill.

When she pulled up beside the little group she realized that stirring Caractacus with a wild gallop was not a very sensible thing to have done, as his job now was to take Theo gently home. He pranced around in circles as she tried to hold him. Draco went to his head and took his bridle and spoke softly into his ears. The horse immediately calmed and stood.

Theo said quietly to him, "You will come, I know, because I have your horse."

"Yes, I will come."

"Help me on then. I need to be home."

Between them they lifted Theo onto the horse's

back. Draco went to take his father's sword but Theo stopped him.

"You will come unarmed."

Did he think Draco would kill them all on the way home and gallop away on his horse? Minna wondered. A Roman solider was taught to think of every contingency. Yes, it would have been easy for Draco. Benoc was carrying Theo's sword but had no idea how to use it. She could see already that Benoc was jealous of Draco because of Theo's care for him. Theo and his three disciples, she thought, and smiled.

Theo was close to fainting from loss of blood and the gates could hardly come soon enough. But they arrived to find his guard lined up inside under the command of his chief centurion Antonius, about to march. Antonius sprung them to attention and came forward, horrified.

"We were about to mount a search, sir. Tiberius has been here looking for you, and ordered us out. But it looks as if you have done alone what he ordered us to do."

"Wiped out Cintus? Yes, he is dead. And the girl is saved. Tiberius was careless in his commands as to the girl's safety, which is why I took it into my own hands."

"I think you are in deep trouble, sir."

"Yes, I know that. You are ripe for promotion, Antonius, eh?" He raised a wan smile. "I only want my bed now and that old fool the surgeon – at least it is too early for him to be drunk yet – and Tiberius can visit me at his leisure. Send word to him that my mission was successful, even though I disobeyed him."

"I will, sir. The gods grant you your strength back. We shall miss you."

He stepped back, saluting, and Caractacus moved on to the gates of Theo's villa.

"What does he mean, he will miss you?" Minna asked.

"Disobedience to authority is a sin, Minna – a sacking is certainly to be expected, possibly accompanied by a stripping and flogging or an execution. We will await with interest."

"Theo!" For a moment she thought he was joking. Then, by the look on his face, she knew he was not. Was she responsible for this horror too, after she had thought her misdemeanors now all accounted for? She went to him as he slid off the horse's back, but he waved her away.

"Go back to Julia," he said. "She is very worried about you."

His voice was now faint, and the two boys had to support him, half-dragging him into the house.

XV

Minna thought the days would never end. The high lovely days of summer, and she immured in the city, in the dust and the dirt and the noise of the streets, or in the stultifying, gossiping servants' quarters of the villa: she was never happy, fretting for the smell of the sea, the sharp sand of the beach beneath her toes, the smell of the wide marshes that ran into the sea with the cry of the gulls and the curlews echoing and the sky – the sky! – wide and pure over the sea right down to the glittering horizon…how she pined! She pined for her horse Silva whom she rarely saw and for Theo whom she never saw. And cursed herself for her ingratitude. She had a job, didn't she? And a kind mistress and good food – what more could a peasant girl like herself expect in this life? She could have stayed in Othona and had the beach and the sea and the sky, yet when she had them she couldn't wait to get away. Was she born discontented?

But mainly she despaired of what her idiocy had done to Theo. Suspended from duty, his place (and villa) taken by Antonius, he was said to spend most of his time gambling and drinking, awaiting the punishment Tiberius couldn't make up his mind about. Tiberius knew that it was more than his own popularity would stand to deal with Theo as he deserved, to humiliate him publicly, for Theo was an uncommonly popular figure. Minna guessed that Tiberius was trying to think of a way of sliding Theo away into the far distance, without giving him the plum he most desired which was to take his men north to fight. That would be rewarding him, not punishing him. Tiberius was a notorious ditherer as Julia pointed out one day at dinner, when Minna was serving and able to hear the conversation.

"Theo will be ruined the way he is carrying on at

the moment," Julia said. "You ought to make up your mind about him."

"I was giving him time to get over his wounds."

"He's over them now, although he'll never be quite as handsome as he was before with that scar over his eye. Come on, Father, take pity on him! He's much too good a soldier to waste."

"I can't reinstate him. I was thinking of sending him back to Othona. Octavius is old enough to retire."

"Well, that's as humiliating as a public flogging. To go back in disgrace! Would you do that to him?"

"Yes, I would. He disobeyed me."

"He killed Cintus, which is what you wanted."

"Don't argue with your father, Julia!" her mother interceded. "You young people don't know your place today. I would never have dared speak to my father the way you speak to yours."

Julia went into one of her famous sulks, but Minna was fascinated by what she had heard. When she was helping Julia undress to go to bed later, she said, "Do you think your father will send Theo back to Othona? I couldn't help hearing what he said."

"It sounds like it. I know he wants him to work here in the offices, but even he is not so stupid that he can't see how ill-suited Theo is to life at a desk. He is promoting my Probus, luckily, because he knows I'm set on marrying him."

Minna guessed that if Theo was sent back to Othona, officially in disgrace, the true story of his killing Cintus in a single-handed fight would certainly have preceded him. He would secretly be everyone's hero. With luck her own involvement in the story would not be common knowledge. Or would it? But either way Theo would hate it.

But Julia's intercession bore fruit. Theo was officially called to Tiberius's villa and given his marching orders. Tiberius's own ship would take him to Othona on the next day's tide. He could take his own slaves and servants but nothing else, not even a horse. Antonius was to be his successor, and was to take over his bodyguard. This last direction caused close enough to a mutiny on the part of the guard, who had been with Theo since his first promotion at Othona. Several of the men had served his father. They were *his* – Tiberius's crass lack of perception made him despised among the whole army. All the men in the barracks were disgusted by Theo's treatment. Antonius was a good man and popular, but hadn't Theo's intelligence and charisma.

Minna was desperate to speak to Theo before he went. She was in two minds whether to leave Julia's employment and go back to her parents in Othona to be near Theo, but guessed that her clinging on to him like this might annoy him. She had done him enough harm, and he could well by now be glad to see the back of her. And besides, she would be forced to marry Esca if she went back home, a fate worse than death. But she must say goodbye to Theo, at least.

She tried to tell herself that he was not going far, only across the river mouth. He wasn't marching away into terrible danger, to fight on the infamous wall against the barbarians in the North. That would make her cry indeed. But her spirits were at rock-bottom as, no doubt, were Theo's.

The sympathetic Julia excused her duties in the afternoon so that she could go and find Theo. By evening he would probably be drinking with his friends for the last time and she wouldn't dare approach him then. She found Benoc in the market, very cast down.

"I've gotten used to life in the big city," he said. "I don't want to go back to Othona."

"I want to see Theo before he goes. Where is he?" Minna could not waste time with Benoc's lamentations.

"Talking with Antonius in his villa – his old villa, Antonius's now."

"Will he see me, do you think? He *must*. I must say goodbye to him."

"Why not?" Benoc gave a sly smile. "Perhaps he'll take you as a slave. I will swap places with you."

"Don't be stupid!"

Minna was not in the mood for teasing, and left Benoc abruptly, making for the barracks. Luckily, as she reached the gates of the villa, she found Antonius and Theo together. Antonius was just leaving. Theo was dressed casually in an old tunic and looked unkempt, a beard beginning to grow. The scar over his left eye was still livid and ugly and not entirely healed. He was lucky, Minna supposed, not to have lost the eye itself, which was as sharp and questing as ever under the cloven brow, fixing her with what she saw as an amused, not unfriendly welcome.

"So, has my little bird come to sing goodbye?"

"I don't want you to go!"

"That makes two of us, Minna. But what can we do about it?" He shrugged.

"It's all my fault," Minna wailed, "making you steal Caractacus! I am so sorry, Theo. I would rather have died than done this to you!"

"Oh, come, Minna. It was of my own choosing, surely? I'm not blaming you. It's a pity I can't take the horse though, so hard-won." He laughed.

"Has he forbidden it?" Minna asked.

"He has. I go alone, with Benoc, and four servants, none of whom want to go naturally. A sad party, Minna. If he had allowed me my bodyguard I would go with better grace. But as he has denied me my bodyguard, my own trusted men, he will live to regret it. I will make sure of that."

"How?"

"I'm not telling you my plans, Minna!"

"You will come back?"

"Be patient, Minna. I shall get what I want, God willing, and you will know of it, but for now I am a disgraced centurion, my tail between my legs. I shall play my part nobly."

He grinned and Minna burst into tears. She could not help herself. And Theo took her in his arms and held her against him, stroking her hair and saying softly, "Don't cry, little Minna. Everything will be all right. Don't cry."

His tenderness made her sob more. The feel of his arms around her was so heart-warming, even if it was an ending, as good as a farewell...she wanted it to last forever, the sweet darkness and the smell of him as she buried her face in his tunic, and his voice soft right beside her ear. She had never been so close to him before.

But it was fleeting. He gently disentangled himself and put his hands on her shoulders and said, "Be brave, Minna. I won't forget you. Look after the horses. I have told Antonius to give you access to both of them, and he is in charge now. He will be good to you. And be a friend to Draco if you can. I would take him with me, but it's another thing forbidden. I just pray he won't desert. He has the makings of a great soldier. So many things left unfinished..."

The farewell was over, and Minna stepped back, swallowing her tears. She had to be as brave as Theo, facing his return to Othona. She managed a smile. Then turned and ran, sobbing her heart out.

The high tide the next day was in the morning. Minna did not even ask permission to go down to the quay.

She went. If Julia dismissed her, she would not care.

Then she saw Theo as she would always remember him: not yesterday's unkempt, disgraced soldier, but Theo the vanquisher of Cintus, the beloved of his men, the leader of his cohort, walking proudly, alone, down to the waiting ship, dressed in full uniform with helmet and sword, the metalwork gleaming in the sunshine. His bodyguard formed two lines of six men each on either side of the road. He stopped and shook hands with each man, then went on to the quay and stepped aboard. Benoc and his servants were already waiting for him, looking very glum. The ship's captain came forward and greeted Theo warmly, the crew cast off their warps and a sail was unfurled to a fair wind from the west. The ship slipped easily away into the deep channel, eager as a dog let off the leash.

A fair number of bystanders had gathered to watch Theo's departure. Minna stood among them, unseen. When the ship started to move someone shouted out a farewell, and a ragged cheer went up, and then the bodyguard let out a full-throated roar, throwing up their shields and beating on them with their swords, displaying their allegiance in no uncertain manner.

If Tiberius had been there, he would have realized what a big mistake he had made.

Minna stayed until the ship was out of sight.

Then she made her way slowly back up the hill to the house of the legate.

XVI

Minna had little time off now that Julia was planning another wedding, to Probus this time instead of to Theo. The atmosphere in the legate's house was strained, Probus being a poor substitute for Theo. But Theo was in disgrace and Julia was a difficult girl to cross when she wanted something. Tiberius opted for the quiet life. That Julia was in love with the young scribe was undeniable: she sang, she laughed, she filled the house with her happiness. Grumpy Tiberius kept out of her way but Minna was helped slightly by her mistress's sympathy.

"Come, Minna," Julia said kindly, "Theo is too fine for you, and for me too. He would be terrible to live with. I know you love him, but Theo is too ambitious to let a woman get in his way. You must forget him."

"I would never be worthy of him, I know that. Of course I'm not good enough for him. I'm only a servant. But it makes no difference to how I feel."

"No. We love the wrong people. My parents think Probus isn't good enough for me, but I am lucky. They are kind enough to allow me my way."

"I brought disgrace to Theo. How can I live with that?"

"Most people around here think he's a hero, killing Cintus. My father made a wrong judgement, sending him away. Everyone says so."

Minna was aware that this feeling was general, both in the streets and in the army. When she went to visit the two horses she learned the gossip from the old army groom, Lucius, who cared for them. Mostly the horses were turned out in a field beyond the barracks, but Lucius brought them in during the heat of the day and kept them groomed and shod. He was training them both to go in harness so that they would be more useful.

"We're not cavalry here, and the gov'nor's not a riding man, only if he has to. But that young soldier – Cintus's son – he comes when he's off duty and he rides out the chestnut. I think it's only his love for that horse that keeps him here. I'm always half-expecting him to ride off and not come back."

"He's nowhere to go now his father's dead," Minna said.

"He doesn't take orders kindly. But he's a great swordsman for a boy and his brain's as sharp as his sword. He'll get promotion as soon as he's old enough."

So Draco was bowing down to army life, Minna thought, as she was bowing down to being a lady's maid. They had no choice. She would contrive to meet him when he came for Caractacus and see if he was still the prickly, arrogant boy she remembered. But their joint experience, tied to each other while their fate was decided by the sword, had softened their enmity, she thought. Far better to have him as a friend than as an enemy; they had shared enough together to start understanding each other. And his love for Caractacus endeared him to her. She understood that part of him all right.

The summer dragged on. Minna's spirits did not lift. Only on the rare occasions when she got to ride out on Silva did she feel the old love of life stirring. If only she could forget Theo! If only he had gone back to Rome, out of her life altogether, then she felt she could throw off this terrible yearning. But on a clear day when she rode out she could make out the silver thread of the estuary and the smudge on the horizon that was Othona, and she rode toward it as if drawn by an invisible thread, like a fish on a line, Theo a magnet to her tingling frame. What was he doing? Had he forgotten her completely? And then she felt sick for her family, her brisk, kindly mother, her stupid brother Cerdic and his dog, their snug quarters behind the blacksmith shop, the old life that she had been so impatient with when she had been there! What was the matter with her, that she was never satisfied? If it wasn't for the horror of being married to Esca, she would have taken Silva and ridden back. She felt she was a deeply flawed person. No wonder Theo didn't want her! Yet he had never been unkind. If he had spurned her instead of comforting her, she might well have forgotten him by now.

Julia's parents wouldn't let her marry Probus until

the following spring, in spite of the fact that she was now really old for marriage, nearly nineteen. They were hoping she might get tired of him, but of course their disapproval spurred her love.

The summer slipped into autumn. Minna never met Draco when she rode out, mainly because Draco rode late in the day when he was off duty. His fellows went drinking and gambling after an arduous day's training, but that was when Draco spent his time with Caractacus. Whereas Minna's rare chance of freedom was generally in the early afternoon after she had waited on lunch, and Julia went gossiping or shopping afterward with her friends. In the evening – Draco's time – Minna was always busy.

But one day everything changed.

It was a sweet, still afternoon. The sun shone but there was a sharpness in the air, the first hint of winter. Minna went out to the field and brought the two horses into the stable. They were housed in the private stables of the commander's villa, not in the barracks, so Minna did not have to run the gauntlet of whistling soldiers, for which she thanked her gods. Without

Theo's protection she felt more threatened these days, a girl on her own around the barracks.

Lucius brought her bridle and back cloth and put them on and quietened Caractacus with a feed to stop him from making a fuss as his companion was ridden away. Minna had learned to take a back way out of the city where she was inconspicuous, and soon she was out in the woods making, as always, south toward the distant gleam of the sea. Today she had plenty of time as Julia had gone to a party and her parents were going out to dine, so she was off duty until morning. When she was on Silva her cares always fell away. His winter coat was just starting to come in, paler than his steely summer gray, with still paler dappling on his shoulders and quarters. In a few years he would be white, not a good color for an army horse.

She galloped, she sang, she shouted greetings to the old women herding sheep and the boys picking apples and the river came glittering nearer and nearer, still wide from the sea. A little boat was being rowed up on the tide. Minna pulled up and watched it, fascinated by the gangly figure who rowed so easily, so professionally... It was surely her old friend Stuf?

Even from so far away she felt sure she recognized him. Or was it wishful thinking?

She put Silva into a canter again, down to the river, and to her joy the rower saw her, dug in his oars to back-paddle and swung the boat toward the bank.

"Minna!"

She was right. It was Stuf. In a few moments he had grounded the boat and jumped ashore into the reeds, dragging the painter after him.

"Stuf! How wonderful! What are you doing so far from home?"

"And you, so far from the city?"

It was like old times, sitting on the shore, catching up with the news. Silva grazed, the boat lay grounded, and Minna plied Stuf with questions about Othona, about her parents and her brother and – of course, but not too quickly – about Theo.

"You can guess – surely – that he's not just sitting around looking out for the odd pirate ship," Stuf told her. "He's been to Londinium and appealed to Flavius Martinus himself for a command to take north. Over the head of Tiberius, that is. And since he met Martinus he's been in a much better humor, so it looks as if he thinks he'll get what he wants -- that is, to take a volunteer force from Othona, and from his old command in Camulodunum – his bodyguards in particular – and march up to the wall. Reinforcements are much needed, from what we gather. Well, we all know that's what he's always wanted. He thought he was going to get it when Tiberius came that time – we all thought it, didn't we? And how disappointed he was. He's been very tight-lipped about what's brought him back to Othona, but the story's gone around…"

Stuf looked inquiringly at Minna and laughed. Minna felt the color flooding her cheeks.

"They say it's to do with you," Stuf said.

He obviously expected to hear something more from Minna, but Minna found it hard to reply.

"He saved my life," she muttered at last. "He disobeyed Tiberius's orders. Tiberius would have let me die."

"Oh, I'd have done that, saved your life," Stuf said cheerfully. "Let you die indeed! What was the man thinking of?"

Luckily, Stuf, making a joke of it, inquired no further. He could see Minna's distaste for the subject. He said, suddenly, putting Minna into complete confusion, "If

Theo takes an army up to Caledonia, I've a good mind to go with him."

"Join the army! But you always said—"

"No. Not join the army. Just as a hanger-on, in the baggage train. I can hunt and find food better than any of those army boys, look after the animals – easily pay my own way. I'd be quite independent. Theo would turn a blind eye, I'm sure."

Minna looked at him curiously. He had always been his own person, living the hardest life off the land. He might not be able to handle a sword, but he could out-soldier many an army man when it came to surviving, and thriving, in tough conditions. And in spite of his hard life, he had the natural manners of an educated person. He was intelligent and well-informed and kept himself clean, even shaved, which was a difficult job even for a man with a slave to do it. Looking at him, seeing his familiar friendly blue eyes, feeling his warmth toward her, she knew he was still the good friend of her childhood, someone she could always rely on. But was he going to go away too?

"I suppose I'm bored, ready to see more of life," he said. "That's why I've thought about it. But I don't really want to travel on my own, too afraid, I suppose.

And I know I couldn't take orders from anyone, so I couldn't join the army if I wanted to. I've been my own man for too long. It's just an idea, if Theo goes."

"You really think Theo will be going?"

"Yes. Theo always gets what he wants in the end. I think it will be decided soon."

Minna tried to put this disturbing news out of her mind, not wanting Stuf to feel that all she thought about was Theo (even if it was true). They chatted for some time: Stuf said he was here across the estuary to see if there were better pickings in this river than on the Othona shore, more salmon perhaps, or possibly an otter or two to snare for a change. He was tired of goose and eels.

Soon he had to move on to catch the tide, and Minna caught Silva again and rode back up the hill, watching Stuf's sturdy figure expertly handling the little boat back into the current. She was warmed by the meeting, knowing that he was a real friend. But his news of Theo was deeply disturbing. There was no one she was friendly with in the barracks to ask if they had heard the gossip. Lucius did not mix with the soldiers. But Draco might know. She was determined to try and speak to him. Her opportunity came when, one evening, Tiberius and his family went out to dine with friends, and she, after helping to dress Julia and do her hair, was given the rest of the evening off.

Covering herself with a cloak and hood, she went down to the stables. To her relief she found Silva alone, and was happy to stay talking to him until Draco might appear with Caractacus. She buried her face in Silva's mane and whispered all the things she dare not say to anyone else, and Silva lipped kindly at her hand. She wept a few tears, and was still snuffling when she heard the clatter of hooves in the yard outside.

Draco led Caractacus in. He was startled to see her and stopped in his tracks, while the two horses whinnied greetings to each other as if they had been parted for weeks.

Minna did not know what to say, feeling the color washing up into her cheeks with embarrassment as Draco stared at her. She wasn't used to seeing him in army uniform and had never felt easy with him at the best of times.

"What do you want?" he asked roughly.

He was no sweet Stuf.

Jerked into antagonism, Minna decided not to

waste time beating around the bush. "I want to know if there are any rumors in the army about Theo – the commander – taking an army up to Hadrian's wall. I've heard he's gone over the head of Tiberius and appealed to Flavius Martinus. Do you know anything about it?"

Draco did not answer at once, tying up his horse and stripping off his tack. The horse was very hot, his copper coat steaming in the evening chill.

Then Draco said, dubiously, "Yes, there's talk. He's coming for his bodyguard, they say. And volunteers. Flavius Martinus has commended him."

So it was true! Minna's head spun. To Hadrian's wall, miles and miles away, to fighting, to danger, out of her life forever…the final blow! What she had always feared. There were still tears of self-pity on her cheeks, but she swallowed and lifted her chin. She really had something to cry about now, but perversely her courage banished all feelings of regret for her own state. She knew where she stood and must face the parting. It would be a clean break, like being decapitated.

"I had heard the rumor," she said. "I didn't know if it was true."

Draco said, "I want to go, if he's asking for

volunteers. A lot of us do, but no one knows how big a force he's taking. Perhaps only a century if he wants to travel fast. They say he's too young to take a cohort and he's under a cloud, for disobedience, so it will probably be a century."

A cohort was four hundred and eighty men, a century only eighty. Minna guessed that Theo would prefer the smaller force, to get there more quickly. He could look for promotion later when he had proven himself in fighting. Theo wasn't a man for accolades, only for being where the action was.

With Draco's civil answer Minna realized that he was inclined to be friendly. She said, "I think Theo would take you. He wanted to take you to Othona, with his bodyguard, but he wasn't allowed."

From his expression she saw that this was news to Draco.

"I would follow him anywhere," he said simply. Then he grinned. "Like you."

Then Minna let out a great wail and shouted, "But I can't! I can't!" and choked to stop herself from sobbing like a maniac. She turned and stuffed her face into Silva's mane, fighting to recover her composure. Not in front of Draco, to behave like a stupid child! She swallowed hard, and came up, grim-faced but dry-eyed. She even smiled.

"I shall have to join the army!"

She saw the relief on Draco's frightened face, that she had stopped having hysterics on him. He had no experience to comfort her. But instinct told him to turn to the horses.

"Shall we turn them out? Will you bring Silva?"

They haltered them and led them out into the yard. The sun was nearly gone and long shadows fell from the walls. The horses came gently, back to the big meadow beyond the barracks, walking side by side. Would Theo take Silva? Minna wondered. It would be better for him to go, with his companion Caractacus, and do some work. He was wasted now doing nothing. But if he went…Minna could not even start to think about it. Her world was falling to pieces and there was nothing she could do about it. The last of the sun slipped over the far hills and she followed Draco, shivering.

XVII

The news of Theo's intentions turned quickly into the talk of Camulodunum. He was to march north with only a century of hand-picked men, with orders to quell dissidents on the way, and liaise with the big forts of Durobrivae, Lindum and Eburacum as he came to them. Antonius chose the men from those who volunteered to go: no easy task as most of the young men volunteered. Theo was to come to Camulodunum with his force from Othona to pick up the rest of his small army, and stay perhaps a couple of days, no more, just long enough to organize his expedition. Tiberius was not making him welcome.

Minna heard his wife say to him, "Once he's gone you can forget all about him. Thank the gods for that, he's caused you enough trouble."

"I shall have to receive him."

"Yes, but there's no need to have him dine."

"No, certainly not. He can stay in the barracks. The less I see of him the better."

Minna saw that the barracks were busy with preparing for the exodus, collecting the carts and animals for the baggage train and the equipment to go with it. The picked soldiers were into heavy training, for an army on the move traveled twenty miles a day with the men carrying all their own heavy gear. Their shields alone weighed over ten kilos; their weapons and personal equipment came to another twenty. Antonius was a much lazier commander than Theo had been, and was now anxious that his men would be found wanting.

It all happened very quickly. Theo wanted to get away while the weather was still good, for autumn was now well advanced. The city – apart from the army – was abuzz with excitement over his impending arrival, but Tiberius had given orders that

Theo was to enter the city not by the main gate but by the bottom gate near the barracks. There was to be no triumphant reappearance down the main street and through the temple square.

As it happened, Theo brought his men across by ship and the small army disembarked by the river and came through the bottom gate anyway, as it was the nearest.

Minna heard the news from Julia, who had been part of the crowd who had welcomed them.

"Don't tell my father I was there," she said to the wildly jealous Minna. "I told him I was going shopping. But half the town was there anyway. He got such a welcome, I can tell you. Killing Cintus made him a hero. They all love him." She laughed. "Like you, Minna!"

"Now he's going, I can't love him any longer."

"No," Julia sighed. "They come and go. Don't fret, Minna. There'll be someone else."

Minna wondered sometimes if Julia would ever get around to marrying poor Probus. If only her own love could be so careless!

But she knew there was no way she could go down to the barracks to seek out Theo. Not even to visit Silva now that Theo was in Antonius's villa. It was better perhaps that Theo should come and go without her seeing him. Or perhaps she would see him when he came to face Tiberius. Questions tumbled in her head: was he taking Benoc with him? Was her brother Cerdic in his chosen army? Was Stuf already lurking around the baggage train? Were all her friends to disappear along with Theo? And her horse too?

Her despair was overwhelming. She just wanted it all to be over, for Theo to go and her brain to go into limbo, numb. To forget, as Julia directed. Go home and marry Esca, be a butcher's wife and have ten children…what else was there for her?

But in the morning, Theo had his appointment with Tiberius. He was to depart the next day.

Minna had heard Tiberius say at dinner the evening before that he would keep Theo standing, not entertain him, but give him short shrift. However, when Theo arrived the door slave showed him into the atrium, Tiberius came to meet him and quite soon – such was Theo's charm – Tiberius sat him down and called for wine. Tiberius, underneath his pomp, was kindly enough, Minna knew, and was hardly surprised, for this was the last time he would see

Theo, but when he called for wine it was she, Minna, who was ordered to serve it.

She set the glasses on a tray and picked up the amphora. Her hands were shaking so much she thought she would spill wine all over the table. Theo had his back to her as she came into the room, but he pushed some papers aside on the table to make room and looked up as she put the tray down.

It was not Minna's imagination that saw the shock – a delicious shock of pleasure – spark momentarily in his eyes. He half-smiled, said nothing – in fact carried on talking to Tiberius – but he had given himself away to Minna. It was not the cold stare of a friendship gone cold, but the lovely, fleeting acknowledgement of the old kinship that had existed since childhood, from the distant Othona days, long before he became an army commander and she a faithful servant. The look she recognized. The old Theo. But quickly covered up by Theo, the professional. The commander talking to his superior. He was in uniform as neat and sparkling as only Benoc could have made it, immaculately shaved, his hair closely cut, his arrogant nose and curving lips as lovely as ever, the awful cut above his eye from Cintus's sword closed now but still angry – the disfigurement he had accepted to save her life. *My* life! Minna thought.

She retreated in complete disarray.

He hadn't forgotten her!

And when he came to depart, quite shortly, he said to Tiberius at the door, "Your little servant girl, Minna – may I see her for a moment?"

Tiberius glowered, shouted toward the kitchen door, "Minna!"

Minna came out. She crossed the floor and stood before Theo. Theo held out his hand and she put hers in his. He closed his other hand over hers and held it.

"Goodbye, Minna," was all he said.

Then he let her go, backed off a few paces, stood to attention and saluted Tiberius.

"Goodbye, sir."

"The gods go with you, Theodosius," Tiberius said.

Theo turned and went out. Minna stood frozen. Tiberius put his hand kindly on her shoulder and said, "Go along to your chores, little girl. I think he has made you happy." He smiled. "I hope no harm comes to him," he said.

*   *   *

The morning of departure dawned cold but sunny, a breeze from the west sending the leaves down in golden showers. The departing army lined up in the barrack square in full marching gear, uniforms sparkling, leather and metal buffed to perfection, shields mended and repainted. From the barrack stables came the clatter of hooves and the braying of donkeys, shouts and commotion as the big wagons of the support train were lined up. The remaining soldiers crowded into the compound to see their companions away, some envious, some relieved they were not of the party, the old ones shaking their heads. The wall against the maniacs of Caledonia was a dangerous place, more so lately since the might of Rome had steadily declined and the barbarians were encouraged. Many thought the North was a lost cause and the barbarians were sure to advance: best to let it happen, they said, and not waste lives trying to hold back the tide. But the emperor would not give way. Orders came from Rome, or – since the emperor Constantine had moved east – from the new city of Constantinople.

This time Theo's army was allowed to march out through the town and through the main gates. It was a bold sight, their own standard flying, the home trumpeters sending them off with a fanfare from the walls. Theo marched in front, and behind him in the front rank came his picked men, his bodyguard, all grinning with excitement, and in the ranks behind came the best and boldest of the fort, including Draco.

Minna was watching, for most of the slaves and servants were out on the streets along with their masters. Minna, having eyes for no one but Theo, had no idea if he was taking Silva and Caractacus. He would need good horses for his scouts and for sending messages; it was highly unlikely he would leave them behind. Nor did she know if her brother Cerdic was one of the force, but as she ran to keep up his wolfhound Fortis came bounding alongside, one of the band of hunting dogs that was included in the march, so she knew Cerdic must be there. Fortis recognized her, and pranced into her path, his long flag of a tail waving with joy, and she stopped to embrace him – dear Fortis! Fortis was the love of Cerdic's life, and had joined the army seamlessly when Cerdic volunteered. Good hunting dogs like Fortis were always useful to an army, especially on a long march where scavenging for food was a priority.

"Don't get killed, dear Fortis! Or lost!"

Would he ever come back? she wondered, as she caressed him. And then he was lolloping away to keep up as the men passed on. Close behind came the baggage train: carts pulled by mules, a line of laden donkeys, a raggle-taggle of women and slaves and, being led by two of the army grooms, both Silva and Caractacus, giddy with excitement at this unusual day. They were giving their handlers a hard time. It was all Minna could do to stop herself from flying to Silva's side, stop herself from running to embrace the horse as she had embraced Fortis, stop herself from making a complete fool of herself as her darling Silva curvetted away out of her life.

Heart-stricken, she watched as everyone and everything she held dear in her life passed away from her through the huge looming portals of the Balkerne gate. She was petrified with grief. "This cannot happen to me!" she breathed. Her whole body was shaking with anguish. The crowd was drifting back into the town, jabbering with the day's excitement, pushing and shoving around her as she stood rooted. She could not move.

She couldn't go back!

Suddenly, she was galvanized into action. Pushing through the last of the returning onlookers she ran, gasping with horror at what she was doing, pulled by a compulsion she could not resist. A big covered wagon carrying tents was still lumbering through the gates, bringing up the rear, and she ran up and clung onto the tailboard, scrabbling at the canvas that hung down the back.

It parted and an arm reached out and caught hers.

"Welcome! Come in," said a familiar voice.

Minna landed like a fish face-first into a great bed of tenting. Like a fish she gasped, giddy with fear.

"Stuf!" she whispered. "Oh, Stuf, what am I doing?"

"You've joined the army, dear Minna!"

"I can't—"

"You have."

She put her head down and sobbed. Yet even as the tears ran down her face, a great tide of euphoria was starting to explode in her brain. She was back where she belonged, with all her loves, whatever the future might hold.

Sensible as ever, Stuf said, "You can ride a while and when you've thought it through, if you decide otherwise, you can get down and walk back. Quite simple."

"Of course! Yes I could do that!"

She lifted a beaming face. "Yes! If I decide to go back – of course I can!"

But she knew she wouldn't.

Minna's Journey

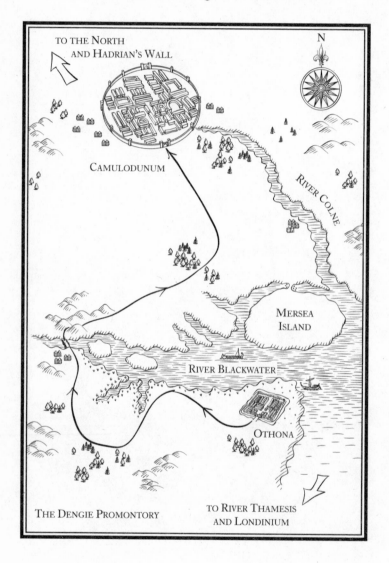

GLOSSARY

amphitheater – a public building containing an oval space surrounded by tiers of seats, used for gladiator displays

amphora – a pottery jar, bulbous in shape with a narrow neck and two handles, used to store and transport items

atrium – the main reception room of a Roman house with other rooms opening off it

Camulodunum – Colchester, Essex

Caesaromagus – Chelmsford, Essex

Caledonia – Scotland. The Romans named the area after the local Celtic tribe, the Caledones

Caractacus – British chieftain who resisted the Roman invasion of AD43. Son of Cunobelin

centurion – a professional soldier, officer of the Roman army, who commanded eighty soliders and twenty support personnel

Ceres – the Roman goddess of the grain and the harvest

Claudius – Roman Emperor from AD41–54

cohort – a unit of the Roman army consisting of 480 soldiers (divided into six centuries of eighty men, each commanded by a centurion)

Constantine I – Roman Emperor from AD306–337

cuirass – a piece of armor, consisting of a breastplate and backplate fastened together, made of leather, bronze or steel

Cunobelin – a British king who took power in the area of Camulodunum from around AD9–42

Dengie – a peninsula of land on the coast of Essex

Fingringhoe – a small river port which served the Roman colony at Camulodunum

Hadrian – Roman emperor from AD117–138, who ordered the construction of a great wall to safeguard northern England against invasion from Caledonia

Jupiter – the chief god in Roman mythology, in charge of laws and social order

legate – a Roman governor, or most senior member of a general's military staff

legion – a division of the Roman army consisting of about five thousand soldiers

Londinium – London

mansio – a stopping place on a Roman road for the use of traveling officials

Mithras – the god of Mithraism, an Eastern Mediterranean religion practiced in the Roman Empire, particularly popular with soldiers

oracle – a priest or priestess who gave advice or prophecies believed to be messages from the gods

Othona – a Roman fort which was located in an isolated area of Essex

Silvanus – the Roman god of wild nature, uncultivated land, forests and hunting

standard – a military emblem carried on a pole

stola – a long dress, that could be worn over a tunic

Thamesis – the River Thames

tribune – a high-ranking official in either the army or government

ALSO BY K.M. PEYTON

MINNA'S QUEST

Minna is just a blacksmith's daughter, yet she succeeds in raising a sickly abandoned foal, turning him into the pride of the Roman cavalry. Her stubborn determination and fiery nature burn brightly in the quiet fort of Othona and soon attract the secret admiration of the proud commander Theo.

But even Theo cannot imagine the part Minna and her beloved horse will play when Othona is threatened by bloodythirsty pirates. Desperate to save her people, Minna risks all as she sets out on a perilous journey over land and wave to find help.

"A gripping adventure, tautly written." *The Guardian*

FAR FROM HOME

Roman servant girl Minna would follow courageous commander Theo to the ends of the earth. So when he sets off north to battle, taking her brother, her friends and her beloved horse with him, she stows away in the baggage train, desperate not to be left behind.

But army life is unimaginably brutal, and it is not long before Minna experiences the terrible reality first-hand. As the battles rage, it seems that everything she holds dear could be ripped from her. And before the dust can settle, she must face the fight of her life to protect those closest to her heart.

Usborne Quicklinks

For links to websites where you can find out more about Roman life in Britain, learn how to make a woman's stola, and see pictures of what Colchester (Camulodunum) would have looked like in Roman times, go to the Usborne Quicklinks Website at www. usborne-quicklinks.com and enter the keywords "no turning back".

Internet safety
When using the Internet, make sure you follow these safety guidelines:
- Ask an adult's permission before using the Internet.
- Never give out personal information, such as your name, address or telephone number.
- If a website asks you to type in your name or e-mail address, check with an adult first.
- If you receive an e-mail from someone you don't know, don't reply to it.